Praise for *Violence Proof Your Kids Now*

"*Violence Proof Your Kids Now* is an exceptional book for any adult who has an interest in clearing out the destructive voice of violence currently inhabiting the lives of our nation's youth."

> —Bettina Ann Grahek, M.S.A., Assistant Principal, West Montgomery High School, Mt. Gilead, North Carolina

"An insightful, interesting, and important book, one that powerfully suggests numerous practical strategies to a variety of different members of our present society, people who want to make the 'violence-proof' concept of kids a reality."

> —Dr. William S. Palmer, Professor, University of North Carolina at Chapel Hill

"During thirty-six years of teaching I have been dismayed to see young people become more accepting of violence in their lives as normal. The usual solutions presented are restricted either to stiffening legal penalties or giving more emotional involvement. Erika Karres takes a giant step beyond by supplementing these with multiple practical actions to counter the tragedy of our children's rising susceptibility to violence."

> —Jim Jackson, M.S. Ed., teacher, Orange County, North Carolina

"This intriguing book is a 'must read' for parents, educators, and every community member who is truly involved in the life of today's youth."

> —Freddie McNeil, M.A., Dean of Students, Orange High School, Hillsborough, North Carolina

"In more than four decades as a priest-educator, I have reviewed more than 200 books on how to deal with varying problems. This book is the best I have ever read. Erika Karres takes a common-sense approach to the problem, recognizing that the whole community is involved seven days a week."

> —Rev. Father Virgil Miller (ret), PNCC (Polish National Catholic Church), Fayetteville, North Carolina

"This timely 'guidebook' will assist teachers, administrators, and parents with workable solutions that can help produce immediate and positive results for families, classrooms, and schools. Principles should consider giving this publication to all of their students' parents."

—Dr. N. Andrew Overstreet, Superintendent of Schools, Danville, Virginia

Violence-
Proof *your*
Kids
Now

How to Recognize
the 8 Warning Signs
and What to Do
about Them

For Parents,
Teachers, and
Other Concerned
Caregivers

Erika V. Shearin Karres, Ed.D.

Foreword by Diane Loomans

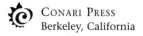

CONARI PRESS
Berkeley, California

Conari Press books are distributed by Publishers Group West.

ISBN: 1-57324-514-3

Cover and Book Design: Suzanne Albertson
Cover Photography: The Image Bank, Steven Satushek

LIBRARY OF CONGRESS CATALOGING-IN-PUBLICATION DATA

Karres, Erika V. Shearin.
    Violence-proof your kids now : how to recognize the 8 warning
  signs and what to do about them / Erika V. Karres.
        p.   cm.
    Includes bibliographical references and index.
    ISBN 1-57324-514-3
    1. Children and violence—United States—Prevention. 2. Violence in
  children—United States—Prevention. 3. School violence—United
  States—Prevention. 4. Problem youth—United States—Psychology.
  5. Problem Children—United States—Psychology. 6. Parent and
  Child—United States. 7. Child rearing—United States. I. Title.

HQ784.V55K375 2000   00-029498
303.6'083—dc21

Printed in Canada on recycled paper.

00 01 02 03   TS   10 9 8 7 6 5 4 3 2 1

This book is for

my daughters,
Elizabeth Shearin Hounshell
and Dr. Mary D. Shearin

And my husband, Andrew Matthew Karres

And for all parents, child caretakers, grandparents,
neighbors, teachers, coaches, and church, synagogue,
and community leaders who are determined
to win the battle over youth violence

And for all the Crystals and Kevins in this country.
They're great kids and deserve to grow up in peace.

Violence-Proof

your Kids Now

Foreword by Diane Loomans,
author of *The Laughing Classroom* and *Full Esteem Ahead*

All children are born into this world innocent. As they grow up, they are profoundly influenced by their families, friends, teachers, and communities, as well as by TV, movies, music, and the Internet. Given the bombardment of images and messages, many of which are violent, that kids receive from the media at very young ages, how do we protect our children? How do we keep them safe from the negative influences that they are exposed to from their peers as well as from the world? We cannot keep them in a cocoon forever.

In addition to the challenges of living in an increasingly violent society, our lives are busier than they have ever been. Millions of parents are divorced or are working longer hours to make ends meet, and more children are coming home after school to empty houses. Children are witnessing direct acts of violence in their neighborhoods and communities, and many are frightened of being shot or hurt at their own schools. What can be done to ensure that our children are safe, and are raised with the loving, consistent guidance that they need? There are solutions to these very real concerns, and this book offers a wealth of practical, hands-on tools and skills to address these issues.

Erika Karres uses her thirty years of experience as a parent, teacher, community member, and nationally recognized school violence expert to identify eight warning signs of violent behavior and to provide seventy-seven practical suggestions for combatting them. As she points out, it is important to recognize the signs of violence not only in your own children, but also in their friends and in the children within your community and schools as well.

Connection and involvement on all levels, from everyone in a child's life, is a primary key. Children must have a strong sense of home and community, know that they are loved and appreciated, and be provided with consistent, positive mentorship and guidance. When we provide these things, we infuse our children with dignity, self-esteem, and compassion, so that they will be less prone to commit violent acts against themselves and others. Erika points out that perhaps just one person could have stopped the tragedy at Columbine.

Our nation's children are our most valuable resource. This is a universal calling in this new century: to be fully involved, alert, and connected to the children in our lives so that we can ensure that the tragedies that happened at Jonesboro, Paducah, and Littleton never happen again. This book is a call to action, and needs to be read by every parent, teacher, and concerned caregiver. Please read it carefully, and then pass it along to another person who has a role in a child's life. Do it for yourself. Do it for the world. And most important, do it for the precious children in your life.

The era of World War II was the most violent time known to modern man. More than 50 million people lost their lives during the war and the events that led up to it. Twenty million of them were deliberately and cold-bloodedly murdered by the Nazi regime. Six million of them were Jews who were especially targeted by Adolf Hitler and his henchmen.

Whoosh! Twenty million lives were extinguished like candles blown out. Like many other people, I often wonder how the world would be different today had they lived. Would cancer be history by now? Would a cure for AIDS have already been discovered? What other serious illnesses would have been eradicated forever? What immense genius, what kindness, what creativity have we lost? How many more Mother Teresas would we have had? How many more Einsteins? How many more Menuhins? How many more Nobel Peace Prize winners?

The fact is, we don't know how much greatness was killed. We also don't know how much good a world at peace could have produced. All we know is that death and slaughter were the norm for nearly a decade in Europe's heartland.

I was born in the belly of the beast of that war.

Indeed, the most violent war years were the years of my childhood. And after WWII was finally over, in 1945, came another decade and more of starvation and violence among the rubble and ruins for the surviving Germans, me included.

Major wars always have aftermaths of hardship and violence. It's as if the blood-soaked earth cries out for revenge; even those still living aren't spared. They too are marred by the killings forever. If you've watched violence wash over your country like a tidal wave and destroy it, and then watched it wash over your family, you too become violent. Or you become the victim of violence.

Or, in my case, you become an anti-violence expert.

My Commitment

I came to the United States at age twenty-one, started teaching in 1967, and have been teaching ever since, first in a public junior high school, then in a high school, and finally at the University of North Carolina in Chapel Hill. During the past thirty-three years I have taught tens of thousands of students, advised dozens of school clubs, sponsored innumerable school activities, worked with countless school committees, and held a myriad of student and parent conferences.

And in the evenings and on weekends, I took college courses on almost every aspect of education, researched burning education issues, and now hold a doctorate in Educational Leadership from the oldest state university in the country. At present I'm involved in teacher training, which gives me an even wider scope of influence because I get to teach young teachers. What a thrill!

But even more important: From the moment I first started teaching I have collected data on how kids can best reach their potential, and what stops them from achieving it. I know first-hand what works best with our kids and what our kids need so desperately.

These days, what kids need so desperately is to be safe, so that they can concentrate on their learning. So that they can reach their full potential. For that reason I have poured one-third of a century's worth of work into this book. We can, we must, violence proof our kids now!

The Wake-Up Call

The Columbine High School massacre woke up the nation to the magnitude of the problem. Until then, many people viewed school violence as a minor irritant, something that rated a headline or a special news bulletin for a short while.

However, the "Mass Killing in the Rockies" changed that. It sent shock waves around the nation and the world. I was one of those deeply shocked. As soon as I first heard about the tragedy, I felt enraged. How could this happen in this country? This wasn't Germany in the late 1930s! Those poor kids and their teacher killed, many others hurt or maimed for life, and thousands of other kids, innocent bystanders all, scarred forever.

That week, in my column for the *Herald-Sun* in Durham, North Carolina, I wrote:

> You can stop the next school shooting.
> One person. A teacher or a guidance counselor. Or a coach or a minister. A neighbor. Just one single human being.
> That's all it would have taken to prevent last week's Colorado

school shooting. Just one man or one woman. Just one single person. Just one.

So where were they? Why didn't anyone see the signs and do something? Because there were signs; there always are.

That's a question that has to be asked. After all, kids don't demand much. Their needs are few: food, clothes, and a roof over their heads. And several more things that cost nothing.

The first thing kids need is attention. They want to be recognized.

"Here I am, world," they scream when they're born. "See? I'm the latest and best human model. Just hot from the manufacturer. Am I not the greatest?"

We have to listen and hear them, look at them and recognize them.

Kids aren't objects to be picked up, admired for a few moments, then stored on a shelf for later. No, they demand attention now—and even more as they grow and become complicated.

So kids need and crave attention. And if they don't get enough in their early years, they'll get it later, one way or another.

Kids also need correction. They want to be shown how to live and do things right. How and what to learn. How to grow up. When they slouch, they want to be told to stand up, and when they mess up, they want to be taught to clean up. Whenever they stumble, they want to be instructed. And when they try something new and muddle it up, they want to be guided into doing it correctly.

Kids need protection, too. Oh, how they need it. Like a roof over their heads, they need to be shielded from bad influences. They need peaceful time to grow at their own rate and not be deterred by sordid interruptions from the outside. Yes, it takes time to discover what lies within, then mature and let one's talents flower.

Would you hire a baby-sitter who curses, drinks, smokes, takes drugs, packs a pistol, and has intimate relationships in your living room as your kids watch?

Of course not. You'd fire that crude criminal slimeball so fast his or her head would spin. Then why do you let TV be your child's sitter? Why let lurid, detrimental and violence-laden shows take over your job?

Parents have to set standards to protect their kids. The same is true for the Internet and video games, CDs and concerts.

We've thrown kids to the lions. And then we wonder. Yet there's no reason why guns and other weapons should rule this country. Guns must be locked up and be out of reach of kids. And gun-glorifying programs must be switched off. That's it. Kids cry out for protection. Let's not withhold it from them.

Kids also need a connection, a sturdy link to life, hope and happiness.

Building that connection is easy. Introduce them to church, sports, clubs and hobbies. Bond them to fun and joy. Let them face healthy challenges and meet them.

Ideally, making the connections is a job for a father or mother, but other adults can fill in. They can help kids tunnel or climb to something meaningful. They can open doors to interesting things. Train kids in a tiny skill that'll lead to a bigger skill. Give them values.

The more satisfying connections kids have, the more secure they'll be. That's why sports are so important and other activities done with an adult, be it talking or tutoring.

All that's left to provide is inclusion—for, most important of all, kids need to be included in someone's heart. It's great when it's their own parent but it doesn't have to be. It can be any human being. Our hearts are big. Surely we can make room for not only our own kids but for others as well.

But we must include our young people. Without inclusion into our dearest nooks and crannies, kids miss the most important ingredient of all—knowing that they matter and that they're loved. And when kids feel loved, truly feel loved, they don't become haters. They don't become shooters.

So, to prevent the next school shooting, all that's needed is one person. Just one. One man or one woman, related or not. A teacher, a coach, a bystander, anyone around.

Just one single soul who cares along the way.

That column elicited tremendous response and was used by schoolteachers all over the area. But what good is a one-time awakening? What good does a single call for action do if it's unheeded in the long run?

Nothing.

So I knew I had to do more. Maybe write a book? I wondered. One day as I was discussing possible chapters with friends at my health club, a crowd of other women, ages nineteen to ninety, gathered around. When I finished, one of them said, "This book can save our country."

So here it is. And whether you're worried about your own child, his or her friends, your students, the team you coach, the youth group you work with, your grandchildren, or your community, it can help you. But it'll do no good unless we apply its message. Just to be upset over the headlines does nothing. Think back to the 1930s and what happened in Europe. What good was a small outcry from a few German folks in 1938 when *Kristallnacht* happened, the night when boisterous young hoodlums and thugs smashed the windows of many stores owned by Jews? When all that broken glass showered sidewalks like broken crystal? When innocent people were killed by the dozens?

The small outcries from decent people were only a blip. But just think of the impact it would have had if all good Germans had united to prevent more such crimes. But out of fear or ignorance, they did nothing. Or because they were too busy with their work! So violence wasn't stopped, and evil took over.

If good people sit back, the bad will prevail. Every time, even now, especially now.

Let me tell you about two kids. You know them, don't you? We all do. They're Crystal and Kevin and live in Anytown, USA. They're your typical all-American kids, and they're good kids, really. No, great kids. When they were born their parents rejoiced, their grandparents beamed.

Oh, how cute they were! How round their little tummies! How fresh their little fannies smelled after their baths and a sprinkle of powder! You could just kiss them head to toe. Every time Mom and Dad looked at their babies, they knew why they had been born—to bring those little darlings into the world.

And those babies grew up beautifully. Their crooked fat little legs straightened; they toddled and got into trouble, but just the usual kind. They were bright-eyed, constantly in motion, always into new things. They gobbled up their Cheerios, slurped their milk, made faces at their pureed spinach. Soon they developed their own personalities. They looked ever more like you and me, like all of us really, as they grew. Oh, this was our chance to relive life.

Crystal and Kevin had so much fun, were so carefree, played

all day long, babbled every new word they could, shot up by leaps and bounds.

Then they entered school, and it all stopped—all those wonderful carefree times. For in school they learned to fear, to mistrust, to hide, to cower. Where do I duck when the first gunshot comes? How will I get out when the building's blown up?

Those questions occupied Kevin and Crystal more than any books or toys. Those worries filled their minds, which should have been devoted to learning. They kept them from being as smart as they naturally were. They numbed and dumbed them! Their IQs stagnated.

How can you absorb new information when you have to be in fear of your life every day? When you can't trust the other kids in the hallway? In the cafeteria? When you have to dart across the school lobby fearing you might be sighted in the crosshairs of someone's gun at that very moment? When you are spending the biggest part of every day in a war zone?

For unfortunately, Crystal and Kevin were born in the school-violence era, a time that let school shootings mushroom.

But no more! By the time you reach the end of this book you will know how to stop the tragedy, how to fight back to restore peace and calm to Crystal's and Kevin's lives. You will become a crusader on their behalf, making sure that innocence isn't killed in this country. You can make certain our kids are not robbed of their carefree youth, that all the Kevins and Crystals in our nation will not be betrayed.

Because you know this: From nothing comes nothing. But getting involved will work wonders. So, let's all rise and act on our convictions. Only then will our schools be safe again. And safe schools mean a safe country, the safe country my mother envisioned as a place out of harm's way. In 1944 she fled Eastern

Europe and carried me to the West and to safety even though it cost her her health. Completely worn out, she collapsed and died in 1945.

Eventually, with the encouragement of my broken father, I escaped to the United States—one place in the world where good is possible. So I know I have a responsibility. A mission!

But it takes all of us—parents, grandparents, neighbors, child care workers, teachers, coaches, church, synagogue, and community leaders. Everyone.

Fortunately, it's possible for all our kids to be guided in such a manner that they will not resort to violence. But we don't have a single moment to lose. Every day that passes brings with it the possibility of more school killings. So let's get going immediately. First, we must learn to recognize the signals that point to an inclination for violent behavior. Then we must commit to violence proofing our younger generation with the same passion and heroism our country exhibited in fighting World War II. We can win this war, too.

We can all work together for the safety of our most precious gift—our children. God has entrusted them to us for safekeeping. And the fact that you're reading this book means you can do what's required.

So let's get all our kids out of harm's way. Let's violence proof each and every one of them. Now!

A New Generation of Kids and Their Families

When teachers take surveys in classrooms today, they find that only 40 percent or fewer of their students live at home with both parents. In many cases, only 25 percent of the student body has a two-parent family. This drastic change in family dynamics has had major consequences for our young.

First of all, the job of raising kids, which used to require two adults, now falls on the shoulders of just one person, usually Mom. That alone wouldn't be so serious if Mom had the same amount of free time as mothers had in the past. But since most of those mothers now are also the main breadwinners—many fathers either are deadbeat dads who pay no child support or are late or stingy with their payments—mothers also have very little or almost no free time to devote to childrearing. And even in two-parent families, both parents usually need to work, and there is precious little time left for the children.

There's no world war going on now, thank heavens, but there's a war raging within our country: Our kids are up in arms. Our young target each other with guns at school with regularity. So our challenge now is to keep all our kids, our own and our brothers' and sisters', safe and to teach them right from wrong. Help them live good, productive lives. Keep them from turning to violence.

Today's Kids

Jonesboro. Paducah. Littleton. What can we do so that tragedies like these never happen again?

We can do what it takes to make absolutely sure such tragedies won't slip up on us. To start, we must focus on our young and how their lives are different from ours were when we were growing up. For the truly astonishing aspect of being a parent or teacher now is that today's kids are a far cry from yesterday's kids. They may look the same and be identified by the same terms, but they're an entirely new species.

Kids of the past followed clearly identifiable patterns. They were

+ first babies
+ then children
+ then preteens
+ then teens, and
+ then adults.

Today they're babies and children only until age seven, eight, or nine. And then? Then anything goes.

From the time kids are in elementary school, they are exposed to adult issues (like AIDS, smoking, drinking, drugs, and sex). This exposure hits them daily like a deadly avalanche in the form of TV programs, Internet access, print media, and their peer groups' wild ideas. Thus, where there formerly were borders between adulthood and childhood, and kids could grow at their own pace in the sheltered space of a stable family, now kids are flung to the winds like flotsam. No more are there segments of life that belong only to adults. Sure, a few of life's slices may still be labeled "adult," but many kids can get access to whatever adults enjoy now, with or without their parents' consent.

In fact, these days many adults blur the lines between what's suitable for grown-ups and for kids on purpose. "I don't want to shield my children from real life," those adults say. "So let's expose them to the utmost in sleaze, gory crime, and depravation." (They don't actually come out and say that, but that's the end result!)

Some parents, of course, don't go that far. But by not making sure certain magazines, TV programs, and Internet sites are strictly off-limits, that's indeed the message they give their offspring.

Fact: Most kids watch at least three hours of TV each day. That's twenty-one hours of possible garbage they ingest each and every week, not to mention the rehashing of those gory or lurid shows the next day with their friends. Also not to mention the time they spend snooping through the Internet in search of something even more outrageous. We all know the "coolest" thing for kids is one-upmanship: You saw a picture of a naked man and woman on the Internet? Bet I can find and download something that's three times more "awesome." So goes today's preteen and teen conversation.

For all these reasons, families today are having the hardest time ever raising healthy, productive kids. And teachers have the hardest time ever teaching their classes. There are so many growing problems that affect our nation's youth.

The worst of these problems, of course, is violence. As a consequence, today all families, child care workers, and teachers need to take a more active interest in the kids in our lives. And because violence is all around us, we can't just keep our own kids safe by locking them in a Tupperware container. And we can't wrap ourselves in bubble wrap either.

No, we must be on the front lines every day, be aware of what our students do on their own, be aware of our kids' classmates and where they go after school, what they do when they aren't with us, and who influences them beyond us. We can't afford to be clueless. It is urgent.

Can Anything Be Done to Keep Kids from Violence?

Yes, it can. Some very preliminary, quick answers are:

- ◆ Fathers, be there and do your jobs.
- ◆ Mothers, set firm yet flexible guidelines and don't back down.
- ◆ Stepparents, treat all your kids well, your own and those you "inherited." Love them by leading them.
- ◆ Grandparents (and according to a recent study, over 4 million of you are now raising your grandchildren, since your own sons and daughters aren't present in the lives of their own kids), your job is especially hard. But all the help you need is right at hand.
- ◆ Child care workers, you're crucially important. Watch out for early warning signs of violence and act on them immediately.
- ◆ Communities, put programs in place for the kids whose parents are errant.

- Schools and teachers, there's much you can do, as is explained in upcoming chapters.

Yes, there are solutions; there are reasons to hope. As a matter of fact, it's possible to stop the effects of all the negative influences our kids are exposed to. We can violence proof all our kids.

But time is of the essence. By the year 2010, there will be an estimated 35 million kids between ages twelve and nineteen. According to research by the Centers for Disease Control and Prevention, in 1997 15 percent of high school students nationwide were involved in one or more physical fights on school property, and 4 percent missed one or several days of school because they felt unsafe going to and from school. Nearly 20 percent of our youngsters were seriously affected by school-related violence. Using those 2010 predictions, that means as many as *7 million American kids* will be impacted by this cancer in our society, and who knows how many others on the fringes will be troubled, tainted, and torn apart inside.

So whether you're worried about your kid, your neighbor's kid, your young relatives, your students, or the young people in your community, this book is for you. We can raise our kids to be whole and healthy, inside and out, if we use the solutions outlined. We can learn to spot the eight major signs of violence-proneness early on. We can recognize red flags and deal with them effectively. The success strategies work. Come, I'll show you how.

All we need to do to recognize a tendency toward violence in our kids or others is be alert. The warning signs of potential violence are obvious.

So let's open our eyes and notice those early signals. We're not talking anymore about one kid getting hurt or two or three. These days, as the headlines and news reports have told us too many times, one violent youngster can wipe out a whole classroom, plus a teacher or several, plus his parents.

In fact, one out-of-control kid can destroy a whole community like a powerful hurricane. Fortunately, the following signs can form a basic instrument that all parents, grandparents, child care workers, teachers, coaches, and community people can use to quickly test for potential violence.

Complete honesty in evaluation is required. The results aren't for anyone else's eyes or for announcing to the world that our kids are perfect. That all our students are nonviolent. That the players on the teams we coach have never had a conflict. Rather, the list of signs allows us to take a hard look at our kids and the other kids in our lives and ask whether they are prone to violence.

Just like we give them their shots or their vitamins or insist that they eat healthy and get enough exercise or make sure they learn their lessons in school, we need to see to their inner well-being. And that includes recognizing the crucial warning signs of potential youth violence.

The Eight Warning Signs

Please, check any youngster you know for the following warning signs. Identify each statement as True or False.

1. This child doesn't listen to, or confide in, a parent or older family member.
2. This child is chronically depressed or angry over a broken friendship, ridicule, or alienation from peers.
3. This child has access to guns or other weapons, or is fascinated by weapons or by fire.
4. This child's grades, interest, or attendance in school are low or dropping.
5. This child's friends are a negative influence and encourage him or her to smoke, drink, do drugs, or have sex.
6. This child isn't involved in church, athletics, positive clubs and hobbies, volunteering, or work.
7. This child idolizes evildoers (like Hitler or serial killers), is fascinated by violent games, movies, music, or Internet sites, or is cruel.
8. This child has no plan for future success and feels that life isn't worthwhile.

If two or more statements are True, please read the rest of this book carefully and where appropriate, seek help. Even one True answer should alert you. It's always best to be vigilant.

If we overlook these early warning signs in our own kids, our students, our neighbors' kids, or our children's friends, we're asking for trouble. It used to be that all we had to worry about was being our brother's keeper. These days we not only have to do that, but we also have to be our brother's children's keeper, and our neighbor's children's keeper and our friend's children's keeper and our community's children's keeper.

In the following chapters we discuss each warning sign in depth and provide success strategies we can use to counteract and overcome the problem.

Sign 1: Lack of Human Attachment

The most significant indicator of violence-proneness in youngsters is a lack of human attachment. All kids need to be attached to at least one caring adult, preferably a parent. Without that human link, they're adrift in a storm, and nothing can save them. There is just no substitute for the most important thing they need to grow up productively—a connection to a human being who cares. Because that vital human connection keeps them safe. In fact, if that connection is strong, the child will not turn to violence.

Like an unborn baby who needs nutritional nourishment through the umbilical cord, a child needs emotional nourishment to connect to the world. From the moment a child opens his eyes, he searches for attachment. The simple sound of Mom's or Dad's voice will make a baby turn his head. Later, the child will recognize the face and figure of his parent. What pleasure it is when Mommy or Daddy comes through the door! Up go the arms so eagerly: Pick me up. Hold me. Carry me. Love me.

It's this daily caring from a grown-up that makes a youngster thrive. Caring is expressed by the way we interact with the child, the way we guide him through the waking hours—talking, holding, feeding, caring. And every little gesture we make, the child soon imitates. When we smile, he smiles; when we laugh, he laughs. We're a big moving mirror image for our children, and they try desperately to copy us. They store away what they learn and later remember it.

Attachment strengthens as it goes from parent to child and back again, reinforced every day by hugs and greetings, by the many "No"s we issue, and by the expressions of pleasure and approval that flash across our faces when our child takes a first step or learns the ABCs.

Older children also need praise and caring comments, loving discipline and structure, and the safety of attachment. A child who lacks adult attachment or who doesn't get enough of it grows up with a deep void. If a child doesn't feel love on a regular basis, his inner growth is stunted. If a plant is shoved into a dark corner without sunshine, it cannot thrive. Without the sunshine caring brings, a child cannot thrive either.

While we're living in some of the best economic times this country has ever experienced, we seem to have let our families slide. As a consequence, today our youngsters are suffering worse than ever before from a lack of vital bond with their parents.

It is reported that parents spend only two minutes a day communicating with their kids. How much attachment can you build up in a couple of minutes? How well will your plants do with just two minutes of sun? Not well at all.

Kids have so many desperate needs. They're bursting with unanswered questions. Growing up has always been hard, but in today's world, it's even more challenging. Temptations come earlier, and there are many more influences that can lure a child or teen into trouble. They see more, hear more, and do more than we ever did when we were their age. Yet, particularly as they get older, we often overlook or withdraw our emotional support. We're afraid to tell them what to do and what not. We tolerate them, are amused by them, and occasionally, are horrified by them. And parents also are squeezed from all sides. That's why our kids are suffering from the lack of human attachment. And that can lead to serious trouble. Fortunately there are early warning signs.

The Signs of Lack of Attachment

Lack of Cooperation

The earliest sign of weak or missing attachment in kids is a lack of cooperation. Not an occasional lapse, as all children have when they are angry, frustrated, or tired, but an ever-present refusal to go along with the wishes and directions of a responsible adult, caregiver, or teacher.

A chronic problem of this sort should not be overlooked. The normal development of a child follows this behavior pattern: Parents and teachers give instructions and kids follow through. And that's what happens, more often than not, when the human connection is strong. But when that connection is weak or disintegrating, a parent or teacher can talk himself blue in the face and the youngster won't cooperate.

This frustrating trend can go on for weeks, months, years. And, as with all the trouble signs, unless properly addressed, it only gets worse. Toys aren't picked up. Homework doesn't get done. Dirty dishes are left all over the house; socks and school papers are flung around. The more you set rules, plead, cajole, or even threaten, the less likely Crystal and Kevin will respond. No matter what you do, even when you scream in frustration, the kids still refuse to cooperate. If they're not connected to you, your screaming is futile. If they're not connected to you, it will only get worse.

Rebelliousness

In the second stage, rebelliousness sets in. Not only will kids *not* do what you asked them, but they will do the exact opposite. Instead of not studying, they soon find ways to skip class or stay out late, or spend money they don't have or visit the one Web site you told them not to. The longer things remain unresolved, the more they push the envelope. Kids at this stage are extremely adept at finding things to do that irritate you or are plain wrong.

Rebellious kids have a million ways to get back at you in anger, and that's what they will resort to. No matter how they appear to you on the surface, they keep building up anger at you and the whole world. Where once they were just laggards, now they're troublemakers. In school, they resort to ever-worsening pranks. At home, if you tell them not to spend time with their good-for-nothing boyfriends or girlfriends, they now do so, and they get pregnant or get the girl pregnant.

Kids who have little or no adult attachment resent parents, teachers, and other adults around them and vow to pay them back, one way or the other. That leads to the last and most difficult stage in their development.

Silence

When children have run through all the phases of being uncooperative and rebellious without resolution, they have only one weapon left—silence. They become sullen, answer questions in monosyllables or with a shrug. I know, for I was such a child. After I found my mother dead in bed one morning at age six, I said nothing for a long time. I was feverishly waiting for her to wake up. Two years later, I suddenly burst into tears because I finally knew she wasn't ever going to wake up. So, I had a reason to stop talking.

But when kids who aren't faced with tragedy stop talking, it's time to worry. When they go from being chatterboxes to grunting or not responding at all, we must become alert.

It is then that they may start living two lives. They may be coldly polite to their parents, throw around a "Yes sir" or a "No sir" at intervals, but sadly that's only for show. Yet they feel they're justified in living a double life. They've tried to make the adult world realize they need a human connection through acting out. Failing that, they have rebelled with as much ingenuity as they can muster to attract your attention. Finally they have become silenced, and that includes the silence of their soul.

Detached kids may do anything and everything. They don't operate with healthy values but with their own misguided ones. They rip textbooks apart, stop up sinks in school bathrooms, and flood hallways. They cut off parts of their skin or pierce themselves with needles to look like pincushions. Or they bully classmates, or torture an animal to death. Or they calmly sit down and plan to kill their classmates.

Separated from the significant adults in their lives, they become hollow human zombies without access to their feelings. They eat, sleep, and go to school, but they're dead inside. And unless identified and stopped at this stage, there's only tragedy ahead.

But it doesn't have to be this way. Our kids *can* be reattached to their parents, grandparents, caregivers, teachers, coaches, and community leaders. Solutions abound. Success strategies are out there just waiting to be tried.

Success Strategies

Push Other Priorities Aside

If you have a kid in your life who seems not to be sufficiently attached, take a look at your priorities right now and reorganize them. All of us have lengthy to-do lists to tackle. Get those lists out now, cross out all the #1 items and write your kid's name in those places.

Do that to every list you create from now on. Your children have to be #1. Always. Even if you already consider your children to be your #1 priority, writing their names at the top of every to-do list will always keep them on top of your mind. From now on your first (and even your last) thought each day must be for your children. Are they on track? If so, their human connection must be good. If not, ask yourself what's wrong with your kids. Then, make mental notes about what you would like to change about your relationship, so that you have a strong bond.

So while you're at work or commuting or shopping for groceries, think about your children, and think hard. Do that until you're sure that either they're on the right path, or that they're not and some change is needed. If that's the case, go on to the next step.

In the classroom or in kindergarten, look at the faces of your students. Are they eager to see you? Excited to be in your care? Bubbling over to talk to you? Or are they silent, sullen, withdrawn, wilted little flowers—dead before their time?

Take Time with Your Kids

The easiest way to reconnect with children is simply to spend time with them. Right now take a sheet of paper and write down how many actual minutes you spend with your children, individually and together, each day. Then, figure out how much of that time is spent on things like handing them their lunch boxes and/or negative actions. Subtract the mundane, meaningless, nagging, and whining conversation time from the total time, and see how much positive time you invest in your children. In many cases, you'll be surprised to learn how little it amounts to!

Next calculate the amount of free time you have. Forget your chores, your shopping, or your gardening. Set aside all hobbies and personal pursuits, except meal preparation and getting clothes ready for the family. Everything else can wait; your kids cannot. Use that extra time to get to know your kids (again). Read with them, shop with them, take walks with them, laugh with them, watch TV with them—even get them to help you with the household chores so you're doing things together. Time spent together is excellent bonding time. It will help your kids to feel comfortable enough to open up to you, so that they will begin to talk.

In school, please find moments to talk to your students when they first enter your room, or in the hallway, or the cafeteria. On the football field while they gather before practice, make personal contacts beyond the lesson, beyond the drills, the sprints. A brief daily greeting especially chosen for a child will work wonders. It's a verbal hand extended.

Schedule Talk Sessions

Kids like nothing better than talking to a parent or trusted adult who will wholeheartedly listen without judgment or criticism. They want to and need to talk about what's going on in their lives. So encourage them. Ask them questions. "What did you do today?" is a good place to start. Then, let the conversation flow in a friendly, caring way.

After supper each day, set aside a planned talk session—just you and Crystal or Kevin. Try to take at least fifteen minutes per child, remembering to avoid critical comments. Pretend you're a tape recorder and take in what Kevin says. Let him tell his day's events any way he can while you encourage him to go on when he's faltering. Say, "Then what happened?" and keep him talking. This is not the time to correct his grammar. Make sure your gestures and comments remain nonjudgmental. You want to let him experience the feeling of being a star in your home.

He is your star. For your child is your most magnificent masterpiece. So don't count mealtime as your main talking time. Of course, there will be talking during breakfast and dinner, but you need to set aside additional talk sessions that are distraction-free. After dinner is the best time for that, as well as right after school if you are home at that time. And be sure to listen carefully to what your child is telling you. Answer whatever Crystal is asking you. If you don't know, say, "I don't know. Let's look it up." Then scout around for the information.

In the classroom, teachers should include discussions on stories read or topics studied and find ways to make sure all kids get a chance to talk. Some kids do better speaking in small groups or just to one person. Or hand the quiet ones note cards with questions you've made up when they first come into your room. It's easier for some kids to read aloud a question than to come up with their own.

Give Attention to the Quality of Your Interaction

As you talk with your child every day, which mainly means she talks and you listen, you want to hear what is being said, and you want to watch how it's being said. Do you get the idea there's something Crystal is not telling you? Is there something Kevin's holding back? Do you have nothing to say to each other after a few minutes? Does your child just shrug and squirm and desperately want to get away from you? Or when you try to move the conversation along, does he stomp his foot and yell, "Just leave me alone!"

If that's the case, don't give up. Say, "Never!" but with a smile, then dedicate yourself to those talkfests. Have some photos ready to show Kevin or a headline from the newspaper that you've underlined and ask his opinion on it. But keep him talking at all cost.

You see, in contrast to a strange dog that snarls and makes you jump backward, when your estranged child snaps at you, you need to get closer. In preschool, kindergarten, or school, when kids are snappy or rude, you need to work harder to connect to them. The mere act of a kid growling at us means there's something that needs attention—now.

Grumbling is a child's cry for help. Muttering under one's breath or constant complaining in class is a student's cry for help. Be persistent. Work at getting closer to your kids, your charges. They need you. The youngsters you look after, the students you teach, all need you desperately.

Reroute and Rebuild

By talking and observing, you will soon know what your kids do all day. In a short time, you'll get a good sense of where their concerns, fears, and problems lie. Ask yourself: Is there any unsupervised time on their schedule? When Crystal and Kevin tell you they're visiting friends after school, do you know for sure that's what they are doing?

And if they are visiting friends, who are these kids and what are they doing? Watching TV with their peers can mean seeing things that might make you shudder. Playing video games can range from harmless to very harmful (more on that later). And, if your kids have access to the Internet without adult supervision, they could be venturing into areas that are not only inappropriate for their age, but are negatively influential. The Internet offers everything from the loftiest to the lowest.

So be conscious of the vulnerable and potentially dangerous times for your kids, and find out how that time is being spent. If you're not happy with what you discover, immediately intervene. Reroute your kids and rebuild more productive ways for them to spend their free time. Make a list of fun activities with them by telling them what used to excite you as a child. Then mention that times have changed and ask, "So what would you like to do if you didn't have school tomorrow?"

Soon Crystal will pour her heart out. She'd like to sleep late, have waffles with strawberries dipped in chocolate for breakfast, check out the mall for a new CD, then, like, send her girl friends an e-mail about her outing.

Of course, you can't let her stay home from school, but she can have waffles for supper and send the e-mail after you've taught her to adorn her correspondence with a fancy border. That may lead her to designing her own greeting cards.

As a teacher, you can assign students projects that are both fun and educational so that kids get truly engrossed in them. Never set a ceiling for their assignments, such as "No more than a one-page report and one poster." Instead, say, "The minimum is a one-page report and one poster." Then let your students get to work and soar.

"Steal" Them Back

What do you do when you learn that Crystal and Kevin are already embroiled in mischief? You go out and fight for them. "Steal" them back. Say, you discover that Crystal has shoplifted a T-shirt. The first time that happens, take her and the shirt back to the mall and make her put the T-shirt back on the shelf. And if there is a next time, serious consequences must follow. But the first time, help her correct her errors. Make her pay for the vandalism in which she has participated. Show her how to delete hateful Web pages. Insist she apologize for bad behavior.

Believe it or not, when you help your child right a wrong, it proves to be a powerful bonding experience. Help your teen quit smoking. Show him how to overcome an academic failure. Haul out your old report cards, swear Kevin to secrecy, then confess: You made a few low marks too back in high school. But later you did excellent work in your sociology class in college. So what changed for you? Go back in your life, remember your past shortcomings, and synthesize how you improved. Then pass those hints on to Kevin. Or remember the time you brought a smoke bomb to school and spent the whole day in the principal's office? Share that experience now along with advice on how not to make those same mistakes. In short, help your kids wipe the slate clean and make a new and healthy start.

In school, never say to students, "Two strikes and you're out." Instead, say, "Two strikes and you're *in*—in my special group of kids with whom I'll work extra hard to make you successful. Just watch me!"

Use Outdoor Opportunities

The great outdoors can help heal any wrongdoing, especially if the bond between you and your child is fragile. So take a vacation now, a trip to the beach or the mountains. The beauty of nature is the best balm for a broken parent-child relationship. The majesty of our natural environment isn't always apparent in cities, but in the country so much falls into place.

A change of scenery and new activities rev up the flow of love and caring from adult to youngster and back again. If you've survived one miserable night in the woods in a small tent with roots poking in your back and a strange, half-cooked fish for breakfast while clouds of mosquitoes descended on you— and you can still laugh with your children—all is not lost. Just get away from everything with your kids as soon as you can and watch the attachment strengthen.

Teachers can show a video of the Grand Canyon or other natural wonders and let the grandeur sink into their students, then discuss how human beings with their full potential realized are even more magnificent. You are here to help kids reach their true powers, one lesson, one day at a time.

Call on Experts

If spending more time together and getting away doesn't help close the gap between you and your child, consult an expert. Sometimes reattaching with our offspring can be harder than we

expect. Of course, it depends on how long we've been uncon-
nected, but in every case progress can be made. Sometimes,
however, a jump-start is needed. That's where teachers, guidance
counselors, and school psychologists come in. They've seen
hundreds of kids who feel misunderstood, ignored, or abandoned by their elders and have sure cures. And if your child's
problem needs extra special attention, they have the resources
and knowledge to refer you to other professionals and treatment
programs that will give you the help you need.

And if you're a teacher having a problem with a child or
class, seek out those of your colleagues who seem to have a
knack to connect to kids. Go to them, sigh, and say, "I can't get
through to my classes. Any suggestions?"

Experienced teachers are walking wells of wisdom. Tap into
them.

Use the Internet

While utilizing the aforementioned success strategies, you can
also gain more insight into creating strong connections with
kids from the library or local bookstore. Hundreds of books on
positive parenting and thousands of articles on parental bonding are waiting for you. Top teachers' tips, too. If you have a
computer, use the Internet (see the Resource Guide at the end of
this book). It puts useful information at your fingertips, as well
as newsgroups, message boards, and chat rooms where you can
gain information and discuss experiences with other parents
and child caregivers who share your concerns. Read as much as
you can, educate yourself, and discover new ways to reattach
with your kids or your students.

Then do it. If you can, send your child a positive e-mail from work. It doesn't have to be long— just a quick "hello" across cyberspace that confirms that you care and that you're thinking about your children. They will be delighted to hear from you. This might prove to be the bright spot in their day. It will also help soften or dissipate any negative thoughts or feelings they might be having by reminding them that someone out there loves them and cares for them.

And all teachers can write nice notes on student papers. All students deserve positive comments on their work, even if their grades are low. Especially if their grades are low.

Always remember: Kids who are praised learn better. And kids who are loved and truly feel that love don't become haters. And they don't become shooters.

The second sign of violence-proneness in youngsters is what I call emotional "unhealth," which is a state between emotional health and emotional illness. We can define emotional health as relatively normal emotions in kids—that is, a state of equilibrium that may move up and down but overall is on an even keel. We can define emotional illness as a serious condition in which one's emotions are unbalanced enough that medical intervention is needed. There is a vast space in between these two states, and it's that vast space that we consider here.

In that space we find various stages of "unhealth." A beginning stage may be a mild, temporary depression that can become more serious, turn into anger, then settle into low self-esteem that permeates everything the youngster does and can have lasting effects. In this chapter I discuss three types of emotional unhealth and how we can respond to each.

These emotional stages are, however, not silent time bombs. They show themselves clearly in the way kids act. So all we have to do is observe the children in our care to gauge the state of their emotions. For example, if a child is forced to do something unreasonable every week (like the sexual abuse or beatings that many kids have to endure today), it's only natural that emotional unhealth would rear its head. It's actually a sign of emotional health to be "unhealthy" if one's surrounding conditions are inhumane, impossible, hopeless, or depressing. Certainly for youngsters to be exuberant when they are being abused is not a sign of good emotional health.

But here we're talking about kids who come from families that neither abuse them, nor degrade them, nor humiliate them, nor use them as slaves. When children come from nurturing backgrounds and do not thrive, we must be concerned. Often we overlook these kids, and only zero in on the most blatant cases, when the family's starving, the father or mother is in jail or mentally ill, older brothers are beating the little kids, and the home life is nothing but chaos.

Either way, we must help *all* kids who are depressed, not only those in circumstances so terrible that it's glaringly obvious that help is needed. The three stages of emotional unhealth don't necessarily follow a progression. Any or all can be present at once. No matter which of the three is apparent, if there is an easily identifiable reason for it—a broken friendship, a "love" gone sour, the death of a beloved pet, or the terminal illness of a dear relative—there is less cause for concern. We should worry about a child's depression that doesn't end or depression without an obvious cause.

Depression

The first stage of emotional unhealth is depression. What makes depression so difficult to recognize is that it can creep in slowly.

In families kids often get stereotyped, if not aloud, then in their parents' minds. Crystal and Kevin are frequently labeled early on as to their personality types. Crystal may be judged to be more outgoing, Kevin to be more quiet. It's when we see those behaviors become extreme or a sudden change takes place that we must pay heed.

Depression in kids is in many ways similar to that in adults, but many adults have learned to manage or counteract depression. We have coping mechanisms in place that have worked for us before. We know how to deal with small and large setbacks—whether on the job or in our personal lives. Not getting a promotion or being otherwise overlooked in our career paths can frequently spur us on to work harder.

With kids, however, fighting depression is a new skill. They have no sense of perspective or proportion. Almost anything, from not getting invited to a sleepover or birthday party, to a new zit popping out on their forehead, to making a B when they used to make all A's in French, can make them sink into despair. And if that despair or that feeling of being down isn't alleviated, it can spread like kudzu and engulf a child.

Warning signs of depression range from "mopey" behavior to listlessness and acting sick. That is, kids who were full of spunk previously now drag around at home, want to do nothing, and seem to have little joy in life. In the classroom, depression can show itself in a student's markedly decreased level of participation. It's one thing when a reserved youngster rarely volunteers, but it's quite another when a formerly outgoing youngster suddenly acts withdrawn and has a constantly somber expression on her face.

Chronic Anger

Another stage of emotional unhealth is chronic anger. This is the syndrome teachers and other caregivers see so frequently in kids today. Thirty years ago, there were fewer instances of it, but chronic anger in children has risen drastically. Today, instead of getting depressed, children often get very angry.

In determining whether the anger is unhealthy, first consider the circumstances in the family. If there are reasons for the child to be chronically angry, then the expression of anger is beneficial. If the underlying cause is addressed, the anger will dissipate. But often children are angry without an overt reason. Truly rebels without a cause, they are furious all the time and don't know why. They are constantly on the verge of temper tantrums or are having tantrums without any reason.

At home, this shows itself by kids' slamming doors or stomping out of the room the moment a parent says, "Hello" or, "How was your day?" At school, chronically angry kids storm into the classroom, slam books on their desks, and plunk down into their seats, arms crossed and with furious expressions on their faces, which do not lighten even when the teacher makes small talk. On the contrary, rage continues to pour from them like lava from a volcano.

While in a few cases a physical reason exists and medicine may help, in most cases kids' chronic anger is a sign that all is not emotionally well. Their anger, which can escalate to the most violent temper outbursts, is a cry for help.

Chronically angry kids are trigger mechanisms ready to explode. When we question them repeatedly and an examination of their background fails to immediately reveal the root of that anger, we must be especially watchful.

The chronic anger syndrome can lead to bullying. This type of emotional unhealth in a child not only affects the child himself, but also others. Chronic anger and ever-mounting rage often make the sufferer into a bully who tries to take his fury out on others. For that reason alone, teachers and child care workers have a responsibility to make note of all bullies and of the kids who are bullied constantly, and to work with both groups to overcome their problems.

Low Self-Esteem

The third stage of emotional unhealth is low self-esteem. It is usually, but not always, a consequence of depression or anger that plagues kids whose needs aren't met, whose cries for help go unanswered. It's really a vicious cycle. Depressed kids don't achieve their best or reach their potential. They languish and often barely get by in their daily lives. The constantly depressed child gets more depressed, since she's excluded, feels worthless, and spends all her time alone. As a consequence, her self-esteem gets lower and lower, and she doesn't know to break out of the cycle.

The chronically angry youngster is in the same boat. He's so busy being angry that his schoolwork suffers. And his outbursts alienate his classmates and make him the object of ridicule or isolation by his peers. Then the angrier he gets, the more well-adjusted kids withdraw from him, the fewer "popular" kids are friendly, the more he gets in trouble in school and fails to do homework, the more his skills slide, the more his self-esteem plummets. That fuels more anger, of course, and so the vicious cycle becomes a spiral that brings the youngster down even further.

We can recognize low self-esteem in our kids by their remarks about themselves. If Kevin is always putting himself down and can never accept a compliment without a disparaging remark, parents and teachers should look into the matter. In school, he may label himself "stupid," be afraid of trying something new, and expect nothing but low grades on his papers. Should he receive a high grade, he might even question the teacher's accuracy. "Hey, are you sure?" he will protest. "I don't make A's or B's. I always flunk." Crystal, meanwhile, will not only call herself "stupid" but will also remark that she's ugly or fat or klutzy, no matter how she looks or acts.

But regardless of how low self-esteem shows itself in a child, it needs the attention of parents and teachers. All three stages of emotional unhealth tend to be entangled and must be treated. In truth, the chronically angry or depressed child often has low self-esteem as well, which will not rise unless this condition is dealt with.

Success Strategies

Identify Causes

The first step is to identify the underlying causes for the emotional unhealth of your child. Just going on vague suspicions will not do, since the situation is too serious. So when you find your son or daughter acting depressed for any length of time, or being angry for more than a short time, or expressing anger often, ask for the reason. If a logical reason is given—"I'm upset because I didn't make the team"—allow a little more time for the depression to lift or the anger to abate.

All along keep talking to your child and asking what's wrong and what you can do to help. Never stop talking. But when neither the depression lifts nor the anger fades, or when you cannot find out the cause for either, or when the depression only deepens and the level of anger only intensifies, go on to the next step.

Rule Out Medical Problems

A complete medical exam is the next item of business. If that rules out any physical imbalance or problem, ask for a referral to a psychologist. It's best to start with a private professional so the child won't be stigmatized as having to see the school psychologist. In school, students are called out of class for psychological evaluations and similar testing, and you want to avoid this. You want to get to the root of the lasting depression and anger, and raise your child's self-esteem, not lower it. All kids fear having something "wrong" with them, so what you want to do is reassure them. You will be fine, you say. We will be fine. Let's just get some help in doing that.

Observe and Report

After ruling out medical reasons for chronic depression or anger, use your observation skills. Turn into the family reporter and note what seems to make your child more depressed or what has her so furious. Keep a notebook on your observations. In today's hustle and bustle, we often forget to write down what we observe. We think we'll remember the important details in our children's lives, but if we are asked later how many hours Kevin spends in his room alone or how many times Crystal listens to the same song with tears in her eyes, we're stumped.

So writing down your observations in a diary is helpful. While you do that, also make special notes as to what seems to lift your child's spirit. Is it a favorite meal? Banana pudding or caramel raspberry torte? A visit from a neighbor? A phone call from an older sister from college? Or a shopping trip to the mall? Increase those cheering-up or calming activities in your child's life. The more times kids rise out of depression or give up their angry stance, the more their self-esteem rises.

Educators also must write down what depressed behaviors they observe. It's not just enough anymore to record a student's numerical grade or a score on an achievement test. Since teachers and early childhood specialists have kids in their care for the major part of the day, they must be aware of how a sad child looks and acts versus a cheerful child. Taking time to note the emotional state of one's students is key. Those observations could be the foundation of getting help long before something tragic happens.

Enlist the School

Since depression and anger in youngsters are so common these days, school personnel know all about them. But maybe your child only shows those traits at home. Therefore, schedule a teacher conference now, and find out how your youngster reacts in school. If the teachers have noticed similar behaviors, you have a starting point. Always remember that school personnel have dealt with those issues for years. Most kids go through periods of either depression or anger, so listen to the teachers' advice. If it turns out your child is alienated in school, excluded from clubs or activities, picked on in the hallway, overlooked in the classroom, or is the butt of jokes, step in at once. Ask the faculty what they suggest. Make contact with the guidance counselor and ask for help, not only for quick fixes but for long-range solutions. Inquire about anger-management workshops for teens and leadership activities and clubs that provide a forum for kids with low self-esteem. Also ask for reading materials for yourself, including Internet sites and handouts. And don't just make a one-time visit to school, but follow through on the advice of the pros. If they have none, find someone who does.

Often placement in another class can move a child out of the realm of a bully. If your child is the name-caller or bully himself, stop that detrimental behavior at once by punishing your child. Do not let him go on with this hurtful action. Kids who are bullied suffer deeply. Help heal them now.

Develop Closeness and Rewards

The best way of getting kids out of a depressed state of mind or defusing it is to spend more time with them. Turn off the TV and other gadgets, and build closeness not only by talking frequently but by doing things together—going swimming, taking walks, going on mini-trips on the weekend, cooking meals, running to the store, or seeing a movie together.

Kids whose parents spend little time with them are almost "set up" for emotional unhealth. The angriest kids in the country are those who haven't had enough attention from their parents or who *think* they haven't had enough attention. Depressed kids also feel they're not worth the effort of their parents. They have internalized the feeling of being not as good as others, thus their low self-esteem. Certainly kids who are angry all the time are furious with the world for ignoring them. They're desperately hoping their parents will notice them and devote more hours to them. Often they do something outrageous just to get caught before it's too late.

In school, kids start with rubbing Vaseline on staircase banisters, then pour glue into locks, then moon others in the hall, then use veiled threats as greetings. *Doesn't anybody care enough about me to make me stop?* is their true message.

Yet what makes it so hard to get closer to students like those is that depressed and angry kids are no fun to be with. Therefore, teachers often have to make themselves *like* those kids, and parents have to force themselves to get close. That's done by listing on a sheet of paper all the positive things you see in Kevin. Include his traits and actions that thrill you and those you see emerging in him, even if they're not yet fully realized. Whenever you spot a hint of kindness in him or notice a special talent he has, list it, and think of ways in which you can reinforce those positives in him. Then plan for some time together during which you'll steer him toward more experiences that highlight his touches of greatness.

This process works, especially when coupled with rewards. So for each hour spent working, exercising, or doing good deeds together, a small reward should accrue, which can be documented in a posted reward system. For example, if Crystal is just "dying" for a new pocketbook, have her draw a picture of it and cut the picture into a dozen pieces. Each time she devotes herself to esteem-boosting activities with you, stick one of the pieces on the fridge. When all pieces are up, buy her that expensive pocketbook without complaining. Thus, there's a goal for both of you—for her to keep developing positively and for you to keep recognizing her growth and honoring her progress. In the end, Crystal will be more fun to be with. She may even let you borrow her pocketbook.

Indeed, any child who spends less time alone and stops being so angry all the time can be enticed to continue on the road to better emotional health by the offer of something she would like to have. And each milestone can be a celebration.

Widen Horizons

What is especially helpful in the process of recovering your child's emotional health is opening doors to new horizons. Kids and activity go hand in hand. You can't be depressed too long, whether young or old, when you're busy doing something you like. And you can't give in to constant anger when you're part of a team involved in a fun activity.

So now is the time to scout out community groups, clubs, sports teams, and art programs, in addition to what's offered in school. Find out if Crystal likes drama, fashion design, or sketching, then sign her up on a trial basis at an art school. Find out what makes Kevin tick. Perhaps he likes dinosaurs, rock collecting, or rappelling.

Whatever it is, keep checking for emerging interests and place your kids into activities they like. If there isn't a class, create your own. With the Internet available in your home or the public library, help your child create his own club and invite like-minded kids to join. Make your house a place kids love to come to, by offering chips and dip and Cokes, by always having an open house, by giving the best birthday parties on the block. Anything creative you can do in a positive manner to get Kevin and Crystal more in touch with other kids will help. Kids who have many friends will get a barrage of calls and notes, and get involved with their own age group, which elevates their self-esteem tremendously.

Add Joy

The best antidote to depression and chronic anger in a child is not to remove something, but to add what all kids need: more joy.

Whenever you're depressed, you know what works for you to jolt you out of that down feeling. That's what living as long as you have has taught you. And whenever you're angry, you know just how to diffuse that too. You know that something joyful on the horizon always helps to catapult you on. Something great happening in your life displaces whatever anger you feel.

So get to work and add joy to your child's life. It doesn't have to cost much. Help Crystal spruce up her room, add a few "hot" items to her school wardrobe, buy her a magazine she likes. Cook her favorite meal—all you really have to do is ask her, "What would you like to eat if your birthday were tomorrow?"

The list will be endless. So discuss possible birthday dinners, pick a few items from her wish list, and make sure she gets them or at least part of them. Right now. Cook that special pasta dish or that lemon pie. Or cook along with her. So what if the kitchen is a total mess?

But before that, spend time talking with her about the pros and cons of pineapple upside down cake versus ice cream concoctions and get her involved in all the negotiations. Anticipation of a beloved food, object, or event adds joy. Discussing one's favorite low-cal snacks is fun too. And comparing prices and shopping all over town for mauve ballerina slippers adds more joy. Planning a vacation trip, setting aside time to see a movie in town, going to a concert—all build excitement.

As a teacher you also have the power to pack in fun. Intersperse your lessons with field trips, guest speakers, videos;

hold an outdoor class, a panel discussion, a contest. First prize is a piece of the most delicious pink bubblegum!

Whatever means you choose, you can't overdo giving glee to kids. By adding joy to their lives you're teaching them a valuable lesson: that if one sits back and mopes, nothing gets better. But if you take control, improve daily routines, and add fun occasions, then your esteem grows. We're in control of that part of our lives that's controllable.

We can choose to be happy—and that leads to growing esteem.

Build Confidence

Depression is a sign of hopelessness turned inward. Anger is a sign of hopelessness turned outward. But by helping your child build confidence in himself, he will overcome both. Once Kevin feels part of school again, has some friends he can confide in, has at least one field in which he excels, has relaxing or fun activities he can resort to in times of stress, knows that he can express his various frustrations to *you,* and knows that one low grade or one disappointment or being called a name once or looked down upon does in no way demean him, then he's on his way.

What you're trying to do is inch him closer and closer to emotional health, just as you would energize him with increased physical exercise. By making a special effort to work with your youngsters on their inner health, you teach a lifelong lesson that will come in handy more than any of the school skills you could emphasize.

Rebuilding a child's low self-esteem and eliminating chronic depression and chronic anger is a lengthy process. Yet every day, every week that you're truly present in your children's lives helps them to see wonderful things about themselves. And it will help you too. Nothing is more rewarding than helping your child grow up right.

In the classroom, direct fun activities toward a depressed student. The teacher can start with a small enjoyable job and assign it to the saddest-looking kid: Could you please feed the hamster today or write the date on the chalkboard? Then the teacher can advance to something more complicated, such as running the VCR for the class. Crystal's confidence will build. How nice it will be to watch her later in the year not needing those small perks any more. Nothing makes us prouder as teachers than noticing the progress our students have made in gaining confidence.

And as they reach the sky, so do we—that part of us we gave them to make their growth possible.

Love Your Child and Yourself

Building your child's self-esteem helps you, too, because it builds your own self-esteem. Often a child learns to turn to depression and/or anger when faced with anger or depression in a parent or teacher. So as you shore up the child's inner resources by getting professional help and advice, by quiet observation and recording, by introducing new activities and by adding more joy, your own outlook on life changes. For if your child was alienated, maybe you were too.

Maybe you've been acting depressed. Many teachers are so worn down by their difficult and underpaid careers that depression is understandable, but it should be avoided at all cost. And these days parents have the hardest time ever being parents. Maybe you've withdrawn from society.

Or maybe you haven't truly accepted your child in the first place. Often parents *say* they love their kids, but they don't really love them, especially when their offspring turns out to be nothing like them. When our child seems to be a stranger, looks different, acts different, isn't brilliant or athletic or beautiful or gifted as we were—or thought we were—when we were young, our hopes for our child can be dashed.

Or your child turns out to be the exact opposite of you. The star athlete father has a clumsy, overweight son. The model-slim mother has a big-boned, awkward daughter. The genius scientist has a child with learning disabilities. The popular former class president has a painfully shy daughter who's afraid of her own shadow.

So now is the time to examine your innermost feelings. Do you feel disappointment in Kevin? Is that why you have withdrawn? Are you afraid your kid isn't like others? Isn't what you consider a model child should be? Are you inflexible in your judgments of other kids, call them freaks, weirdos, misfits? Just because you see some boys or girls who don't fit your stereotypes, do you condemn them? Are kids who are outside the regular norm a cause of shame for you? Maybe your child is different. His sexual orientation isn't the same as yours. But no matter who your child is and whatever his traits and his looks are, always consider it an honor to have this child. Who are you to question God's handiwork?

God gave you this child for a reason. God gave us all the Crystals and all the Kevins for a good reason. So put negative thoughts into the garbage, forgive yourself, and forge ahead. You wouldn't have this wonderful child if you weren't up to the task. You wouldn't have these wonderful students to teach if you weren't up to the challenge.

So be honored you have been given the chance to play a major role in this young life. Helping our youngsters grow up into healthy individuals is all the reward we need.

Deal Effectively with Your Own Anger

Sometimes without even being aware of it, we teach kids inappropriate ways of dealing with anger. It's amazing how much they learn from us—not only positive traits, but also negative ones. So we must give ourselves a periodic anger checkup and ask ourselves how we react when things aren't going our way. Are we training innocent kids to look down on other ethnic groups? And on people whose lifestyles are different from ours?

Are we ruining our young? And all for what? Just because our parents told us that was the way to be?

But we're not our parents, or are we? No, we are an improved version of them. Humankind always strives to produce a better model with each generation, and as representatives of that better model, we must stop making negative remarks about other people. We do that by watching ourselves carefully. By making note of our reactions to everyday small annoyances and to the bigger obstacles that crop up. Let's ask ourselves:

- ◆ Do I become infuriated at the drop of a hat?
- ◆ Do I yell or shake a fist when a driver cuts me off, when traffic is stalled, when a clerk is rude in a department store, a waiter is slow to deliver, or I get the runaround in a bureaucracy? When the mail is slow? The weather's rotten? Taxes keep going up? I don't get that long-awaited promotion?
- ◆ Do I seethe when a policeman tickets me, but not the crazy drivers? When minorities are usurping positions

I've held? When government officials get away with whatever they can?

♦ Am I furious when people in power act in a shameless manner? When all around me corruption seems to mushroom?

If we do get angry quickly and frequently, we must do all we can do defuse our hate and anger. Each and every day we must watch what we say and never show signs of racism or prejudice.

Remember, each time we deal with an occasion in a reasonable manner, we teach our kids to be less inclined toward violence. But each time we rant and rave, shake fists, curse, or use racial slurs, we increase their violence potential. We pour fuel on the fire in the invisible war that our nation's caught up in, the war of our kids with other kids and with society. So we must set a good example and not give in to overt rage. The best way we can teach our young to manage their frustration is to manage ours. Make a list of your pet peeves, get to work on those you can tackle, and forget about those you can't. Dash off letters to the editor to air your views, call in friends for a party just to vent your frustrations, look for a job that allows flexible hours so you can avoid the worst traffic. No matter what you decide to do, strive to be at peace yourself.

That means teachers should not fight with their colleagues at school or blow up at students who don't do their homework or fail their tests. As parents, we should never fight with our partners in front of our children. Kids learn to imitate combative behaviors by watching their parents fight and their teachers argue. But they learn to reason and calmly work out their problems if they watch the adults in their world do the same.

In the event that parents cannot avoid fighting, they should have their fights in another room or at a time when kids aren't at home. And if that's not possible, parents must always report back to their kids that the fighting is over and that the conflict has been worked out: "See how we worked out our disagreement and now can go ahead on an even keel?" This is the most important message about conflict parents give their kids: You too can learn to work through whatever disagreements you have with your peers, just by watching us.

Kids do indeed learn anger management best in their own homes. That's where the process must begin.

Guns

The truth is that guns, though acceptable to those parents who keep them, are one of the worst factors contributing to youth violence today. In homes with guns, the likelihood of kids' taking guns to school is increased. There is an increase in gun-related suicides. And, of course, kids who carry guns will use them, if not immediately, at some point. The more often they carry a gun, the more the likelihood of a tragedy.

Guns in the home don't have to become problematic, if parents are conscientious in controlling their accessibility. But without strict control, guns and other weapons are a serious problem. Half the homes in this country have at least one gun, and since our country was founded in part with the power of guns behind it, the presence of guns is so ingrained in our culture that it's impossible for most people to think of getting rid of them. Gun ownership is seen not only as a constitutional right, but also as one of the ways the freedom of individuals is maintained.

Many historians claim that what makes our country great is our right to bear arms. They say if guns hadn't been confiscated in pre-WWII Germany, millions of innocent citizens, Jews and others, would not have been led to slaughter without resistance. They would have fought back and overthrown the Nazi regime. Anne Frank would not have died.

Therefore, many people feel that the first step toward a dictatorship is the disarming of the population, and that simply outlawing gun ownership will not only not work, since the criminal element will not give up its weaponry, but will also undermine individual freedoms. Additionally, with crime on the rise in many areas, a feeling of fear would permeate the country if all private guns were forbidden. And owning and handling guns for sportsmanship would be squelched.

Whether we agree with such views or not, guns are part of the American scene. They have been from the start and seemingly will continue to be. However, our attitude toward guns must be changed from this moment on, for their image and importance have been unduly glorified by the modern media—with terrible results.

Movies depict criminal lifestyles as glamorous, influencing our kids to imitate that behavior. TV shows heavily highlight the use of guns. Similarly, modern music and videos stress the use of guns and other weapons. In the absence of a major war, which might broadcast a realistic devastation of what guns can do to human beings, only the glamorous aspect of guns is portrayed. Most youngsters are not aware of the horrors that made an impression on earlier generations. For them, only now matters. Since they have experienced guns only as a status symbol, a hot commodity, and a possession with which to generate respect, they're more in awe of guns than ever.

Added to that is the Hollywood-created superhero who blasts to smithereens everything in his or her way and the similar characters that appear in many a popular video game. In truth, guns are so much a part of most blockbuster movies that images of bodies strewn left and right, whether on the big screen or the small one, are accepted by kids as a fun diversion and then as an easy answer to their problems. Because of the prevalence of violent movies and TV programs, a gun is seen as the one possession with which today's average guy or underdog can get some satisfaction.

Furthermore, today's kids are much less supervised than in the past. In earlier times, kids came home after school to a house in which Mom or another older relative ran the show. There was hardly any unsupervised time. Also, communities were smaller; many of them had a close-knit village-type feeling, and neighbors looked out for one another.

No more. Now kids often come home to an empty house. Some families expect kids to look after themselves every day during the "dangerous hours"—from 3:00 P.M. to 7:00 P.M.— from age ten on or younger.

That means many kids have four hours a day to themselves when they're either watching guns in use on TV and in movies, or guns in action in TV news reports, or when they are shooting virtual guns in video games. Or kids spend their dangerous hours listening to guns described in throbbing or pulsating songs in rap or heavy metal music. Guns! Guns! Guns!

Is it any wonder, then, when kids start prowling around the house in search of guns of their own? Or log on the Internet to find out the names of gun dealers, the dates of gun shows, and whatever else is out there in assorted weaponry? And since kids congregate in groups of two or more after school, if they can't find a gun at their own home, someone in their group is surely able to get hold of one.

It's not only the easy access to guns that should worry us, but also the fascination many youngsters have developed for them. Indeed, nowadays, many youngsters crave guns. Given easy access, in the course of one unsupervised afternoon, kids can study guns in all forms, just like earlier generations studied their lessons. Then of course, they want to touch and play with the real thing. "Kids get into all kinds of stuff," said one mother whose son accidentally shot himself.

That's correct. Unsupervised, kids do get into "stuff." Indeed, it's not difficult for any youngster to have access to a gun. Many parents let their guns lie around like TV remote controls. Or they showcase them like golfing trophies in the den and proudly display their collection in gun racks, little realizing that the fascination with guns has heightened for their kids. Parents remember being warned of the seriousness of guns and being taught how to handle a hunting gun, for instance, but that was back when guns were unglamorous. Now they're similar to cigarettes, liquor, or marijuana—titillating toys. Thus, no parent can ever again expect to let any of these items just sit around on a dresser or in a bureau drawer with unsupervised kids playing nearby.

As kids grow, so grows their appetite for toys, especially for new and exciting toys. Kids are so smart, they want what's "hot." And guns are very hot.

So parents must lock up whatever presents a danger for their offspring. That includes all guns. Furthermore, unsupervised time needs to be eliminated. We must worry about whether other kids in the neighborhood or our children's friends are being properly supervised. For when any child, no matter how far removed from us, is left without someone watching over him and with an accessible gun in the house, that child may get hold of the gun. Then horrible accidents can occur. In too many cases, all a kid wanted to do was "play" with a gun or to show it off to friends on the playground or at school. But the end result was serious injury or death of an innocent youngster.

Another kid killed!

So kids must be supervised, and guns have to be made inaccessible and unglamorized once and for all.

Bombs

Being watchful involves more than keeping an eye on the gun cabinet. It also includes screening access to other possible weapons and to information about them, especially now that the Internet has made every possible destructive device visually and virtually available to kids as young as kindergartners.

In the past, recipes for harm and destruction weren't easily available. Few books were written on the topic and were hard to find. Their language also was arcane. Maybe some bookstores had gun books available, but those texts weren't delivered to your home in simplified language, with enticing pictures, charts, and words of encouragement that almost make putting together a mega-bomb child's play.

No more. Now it's high season every day! And even if you have a software program to block out sleaze and violent sites from your computer, someone in the group to which your daughter belongs won't have the blocking device. You may screen the violence out. But other parents invite violence in. That's the problem: Too many kids, including yours, have access to Internet sites that teach them how to make weapons of mass destruction, or how to sharpen switchblades for maximum effect. Kids can easily find out how to make bombs and other incendiary devices.

Success Strategies

Be Alert

This change in our culture permeates the whole country and has turned it into a huge candy store of violence. Therefore, parental vigilance is of utmost importance. Parents must plan for every hour in their kids' lives. On a chart they should list where their kids are and which adult is in charge. Nowadays, with both parents working, often Mom assumes Dad is coming home early. And Dad thinks this is Mom's day to structure Crystal's afternoon activities and take over her supervision. So often, there's nobody when Crystal comes home from school. This type of negligence must stop. We must plan for our children to be watched, either by ourselves or by another responsible adult, and we must always have a backup plan, in case the baby-sitter is sick or the neighbor has an emergency. Or school closes early due to bad weather.

Begin by being curious, by being alert—that's key. Watch what occupies your kids and their friends. Make a note of how they spend their time. Get to know the parents of your kids' classmates. Look at your kids' reading materials, read their essays. When they prepare oral reports or speeches for class, make videos for school, or take pictures of themselves, don't just nod at their efforts. On the contrary, pay close attention to the topics that interest them.

In this instance, teachers have the perfect opportunity. Don't just grade papers for grammar. Grade them carefully for content. Notice any gun-glorifying messages and deal with them.

This isn't hard. Kids are easy to read. If violence is uppermost on their minds, they will write about it, discuss it with friends on the phone, buy magazines dealing with violent pursuits, or clamor to watch movies that teem with gratuitous killings.

So listen to your kids' music, take part in their world, learn all about their culture. Obtaining materials, as well as recipes, for making bombs and for blowing up buildings, cars, or people is a sure warning sign that kids have violence on their minds. A preoccupation with other destructive equipment, like knives or other weapons, is cause for concern as well. In fact, knives are used more often than guns in outbursts of youth violence.

One other destructive force must be mentioned here, and that is fire. That's where child caregivers come in. When kids from early on play with matches or seem fascinated by fire, caregivers must take note. And parents must be alerted. Matches, candles, wax, and wicks in Crystal's or Kevin's possession should alert you as well.

Also if kids cheer at images of fire, violent car crashes, or human destruction, their proneness to violence must be questioned. Kids imitate what they're obsessed with. A child playing with matches, if she is not stopped, will soon light a fire in a school trash can, then proceed to even bigger cases of arson.

Indeed, since violent references and images crop up in so many places in our culture, they must all be examined. And over and over. And every effort must be made to disenchant our youth with weapons and gratuitous violence in any form or fashion.

It's all too easy just to think kids are going through a phase, but when it comes to violence, the phase lasts. So we must keep on being vigilant, no matter what. We have to pay attention to their talk, especially when they're among themselves. Watch their reaction when you tell them you have secured your guns. Observe them when you tell them a term paper on guns is not permissible. If they shrug, no problem. But if they scream and yell about their freedoms and claim you've trampled on them; if they clamor for pistols, hunting guns, bullets, and bowie knives for their birthdays; if they are saving money to buy a weapon for themselves and discuss bombs and bomb making with their friends, you know there's a problem.

Then you must act. At once!

If you notice kids accessing violent Internet sites, drawing pictures of guns on their school papers and notebooks, decorating their rooms with posters depicting guns or slogans, including violent words, step in at once. Just listen with your heart, then you will hear them: Your kids are calling out for help. They're hurting and need you. Now. Or they need you to take them to a professional who can help.

Kids are *not born destroyers*. They're not evil or violence prone from babyhood on. Crystal and Kevin are whole and holy from the moment they're born. They only become damaged goods if we allow it. If we close our eyes as they wander off the normal path and stumble into the quicksand of negative behaviors and pastimes.

I know. Little kids will aim at each other with toy pistols, but they continue only if you, the parent or the day care provider, don't redirect them to a positive pastime. So check on the toys in your house and the toys kids play with in day care. Make sure you know what they watch on TV there and how much.

The signs are obvious when kids are preoccupied with weapons. Adults may be able to feign disinterest in weaponry when they're consumed by it. But our youngsters are quite honest about their attraction, talk about it incessantly, or display their interest in other ways.

They make Christmas, Hanukkah, Kwanzaa, or other holiday wish lists of weaponry. They spend hours perusing gun magazines, get excited at the thought of visiting gun shows, fondle knives, write research reports on bomb ingredients, blow up small explosive devices in the backyard in the name of a science project. They carry books of matches and play with them.

So wake up and see what your child is up to, what your students have on their minds. See their interest in weaponry for what it is—a desperate cry for help, a plea from a child for someone in the adult world to listen, step in, take away the dangerous objects.

Help me, somebody please help me! Turn me around! Make me a good kid!

How can we not hear our children and respond?

Restrict Access

The next thing that must be done is restrict kids' access to guns and other weapons. You do that by securing every item that is or can be a weapon. Study all the security locks on the market, then use the "triple" approach to total safety. First, buy the best gun locks available and affix them to your guns. Not just trigger locks, but actual locks that prohibit access to the gun and ammunition to anyone but parents.

Second, gun owners must put their weapons into a sturdy closet or safe and lock them up. Keep the combination, which must be more complicated that your birth date or some other easy-to-figure-out series of numbers, to yourself. Don't record it anywhere except away from home, maybe in your office, and there only in a safe place. You want to make absolutely sure nobody has access to your guns except an authorized adult.

Third, make certain that the sturdy closet or safe has an alarm system, so that any tinkering sets off an ear-blasting noise, not only at home but also in your office. This three-pronged attack to securing your weapons is absolutely necessary, not only to protect your kids but also to keep the guns out of other youngsters' hands.

But what about the prowler who may surprise you in the middle of the night, thus making a loaded gun on your night-stand imperative? Scare him away with a loud watchdog, a sound alarm system, a neighborhood watch system, and increased police patrol. While we fear being caught unarmed by an intruder, the likelihood of that happening is remote. However, the likelihood of our kids' and their friends' getting their hands on any gun lying in our dresser is enormous.

If you must sleep with your gun, remove your gun every evening from its extremely safe location and keep it by your bedside during the night in the top drawer of your nightstand. But make sure that drawer is lockable and only you know the combination to the lock. Then first thing every morning before dashing to the bathroom, secure the gun again as outlined above. That will require several extra minutes, so you have to decide if it's worth it. And you have to decide whether you're likely to oversleep, which means you'd rush off with the weapon lying unsecured in your nightstand all day. A clever kid—your own or your neighbor's kid or the kid accompanying the house-cleaning crew or the yard service—can pry his way into your nightstand while you're holding that power meeting at the office. Just imagine coming home to a bloodbath that was caused by your carelessness. Is having a gun handy in the mid-dle of the night worth that much to you?

America's leading expert on security, Gavin de Becker, gives this same message over and over in detail in his book *Protecting the Gift:* Easy gun access is not worth our kids' lives.

Know Your Kids' Friends and Parents

Another important step in preventing or counteracting our kids' attraction to weapons is to get to know our children's friends and their parents. It's helpful to hold cookouts, sponsor family sports events, or make trips to the lake to which our children can invite their pals. Then bring up the gun topic. That way you can listen to the views of your children's friends. Also by socializing with their parents you get a better glimpse into their thinking. The older our offspring get, the more they absorb from their peers. Therefore, it's in our best interest to make the acquaintance of our sons' and daughters' classmates and understand their home situations.

If we find out that the gun safety measures of our kids' friends are not equal to our standards, we have two choices: Convince the other parents to update their security measures, or not allow our kids to spend time at their houses any more, be it at birthday parties or on overnight visits.

Sure, that's harsh. But what would you rather have—your kids' having all kinds of friends and possibly getting hurt or killed? Accidentally shooting someone else? Or out of harm's way?

We can't be wishy-washy about other parents' lax rules. Kids are just too curious. That's their strength and their weakness. So, the more we secure guns and other weapons at our homes, the more we must demand that the parents of their friends do the same. Also, we need to insist on no unsupervised time when our children visit there and on no unrestricted computer access.

None, anywhere—not at school, not in any home our kids visit.

Educate Kids

As soon as all your guns are triple-secured, talk to your kids about the reasons for those safety measures. Explain to them the dangers that guns pose in the hands of kids. For example, an August 23, 1999, *Newsweek* article reports that 4,223 children were killed by firearms in 1997 alone, "many of them in accidents while playing at friends' homes in their own neighborhoods. Thousands more were injured. Some experts predict that firearm related injuries could soon replace car crashes as the leading cause of death" for kids. Read this article or similar ones to your kids, discuss them, and talk over and over about all the lives ruined forever by guns or snuffed out completely.

And if you still insist that your children learn to handle guns safely for their benefit, stress that they never touch a gun unless you're there to show them how. Then teach them in the course of many lessons how to handle, clean, and store guns correctly.

Remember how long it takes for a kid to get a driver's license? Make sure you double those hours when instructing Crystal and Kevin about gun safety. Teach your kids the parts of a gun, the security features, and most importantly, the utmost care that must be taken when handling any weapon. Just make darn sure your children are safe!

Families who don't have guns should assume that the home Crystal is visiting has a gun on its premises, just to be on the safe side, and teach gun safety. From early on, she must be taught to ask her friends without embarrassment if their parents own a gun. If they do, you must make the next move: find out from Crystal's friend's Mom or Dad how the family gun is secured. If there is the slightest doubt about the weapon's accessibility, or if the precautions seem sketchy, it's best never to let Crystal visit that home, unless you come along to supervise the birthday party or chaperone the sleepover. It's much better to become known as a nervous-nellie parent than to have Crystal injured. Or killed!

Reduce Access to Information about Weapons

Along with restricting access to actual weapons, information about weapons must be restricted too. That means parents must educate themselves about the programs that exist for blocking detrimental Internet sites from your home computer, and teachers must insist on the same policy at school. Then install those programs. Move the computer into the family room, so you can supervise which sites your kids visit. Remove all TVs and VCRs from your children's rooms as well, so you can keep an eye on what they're watching. These days, kids complain over and over that they wish their parents were more vigilant. "Please, be stricter," is their inner wish. So don't just take your kids' word for what they claim they're going to see on the big screen. Check on what they actually see. Quiz them when they come home from a movie.

Also, when Kevin stops over at a friend's house on the way to the movie or afterward, be especially watchful. Ask the friends' parents right out: "What is your policy on Internet use for your kids? What do you let them watch on TV?"

If the parents of Kevin's friends are equally concerned about protecting their children from gun glamorization and weapons information, then you can relax. But if they blow off your questions and call you overprotective, restrict Kevin's access to those friends. Again, it's better to be too strict than too lenient. This may cause some complaints from Kevin. Indeed, being tough about what information your offspring can pull up on the World Wide Web may cause serious whining, but that's what being a parent means. A parent is less of a pal and more of a leader. Or should be.

And don't ever believe that a term paper requires your youngster to research pipe bombs and hand grenades. Some schools do indeed allow kids to pick their own topics for research, but there's nothing to be gained by giving them a total free hand in the topic selection or in their end-of-class video presentations. If schools don't restrict the topics to something acceptable, then parents must do so, right after they take their complaints to the administration. No child should ever be allowed to study, read, write about, and present to their classmates a school project on weapon making. Or on how to kill teachers and classmates. Or on the "fun" of shooting one's parents, then committing suicide.

Or on the "joys" of wiping out 250 of their peers.

Hold Periodic Safety Checks

Just as we hold periodic fire drills and check our homes for security purposes, and just as we take our kids for annual checkups and dental appointments, so we must now do one more thing—periodically check our houses, yards, garages, workshops, beach and mountain cottages, and yes, our kids' rooms, for hidden weapons. And we must insist our neighbors and all the parents we can contact do the same, or else we must not allow our kids to visit.

And remember this: Some parents do lock up their guns, but over time they become careless. Others move and forget to install new safety measures. Or they buy yet another hunting gun or add to their collection of dangerous knives without securing their latest purchases. Or they teach their eldest daughter how safely to handle a handgun, then forget to instill the same skills into their younger kids. Or they divorce and remarry, a process by which they become dads or moms to a brand-new set of kids. Then they get so busy just adjusting to new family parameters that they totally forget to include the new siblings in the most important lessons they can ever provide: that is, to respect guns and to stay away from them. And to report back to their parents when other kids have access to guns.

At school, kids must be taught to report immediately any classmate who brags about having a gun or access to one. Metal detectors must be placed at all school entrances, and not only at those leading to the gym or the stadium, as is common practice in many middle, junior, and high schools today.

Reduce Unsupervised Time

There's no denying it: We adults are busier and busier. So our kids are left more and more on their own. But we can't let that happen. The less unsupervised time our kids have, the less likely they are to become embroiled in a fascination with guns and violence. Therefore, parents and teachers must plan ahead.

That means someone must be available to look after our kids after school, whether that's inconvenient or expensive or not. No youngster should be home alone without a responsible adult around, even if he is older—say, thirteen or fourteen. While kids mature earlier these days, in gun matters they remain naive and are slow to grasp the dangers.

So it's best to schedule our kids' after-school time with all kinds of activities that provide healthy thrills and joys. Boredom and lack of supervision are two factors that must be avoided at all costs. And a network of safety must be thrown around all youngsters. Why not hire a retiree to provide extra supervision after school? We have school-crossing guards, don't we? Now we need after-school protectors for all our kids.

Work Toward a Peace Culture

Much can be done by guiding a youngster's interest away from violence and toward activities that deal with peace. Books can be supplied for that purpose, TV shows can be watched as a family and discussed. Unnecessary violence must be talked about and be presented as the horror it is.

Visit community organizations that are devoted to peace. Obtain pamphlets and other handouts from these centers and peruse them. Then you can steer discussions around the supper table to the topic of nonviolence. TV news-watching should taper off as well. Most news programs revel in too much bloodshed and crime. By emphasizing peace, kids will feel a revulsion toward guns and other weapons as they grow up discussing alternative ways of settling their conflicts. As they learn to rise above fighting.

Each parent who purposefully redirects her kids toward a nonviolent outlook does her share to turn our whole country away from the prevalent violence culture. We do that by expressing our negative opinions on violence. We show our interest in peacemaking as much as we can. We demonstrate that we mean it by making contributions to peace-promoting causes and organizations, such as local conflict mediation or arbitration groups. A look in the phone book will steer us in the right direction.

As far as schools are concerned, in every one of them, from elementary to college level, educators must establish peer conflict resolution clubs. In the early grades, teachers must lead the peacemaking activities. But from middle school up, students should be trained so that they themselves become peer mediators and can resolve whatever conflicts arise. Even in a school where little conflict exists, a strong commitment to nonviolence must be made by the staff, so that kids are convinced from early on that all disagreements can be settled without fighting.

This way, parents, child caregivers, grandparents, teachers, and leaders everywhere can guide our youth toward attitudes of peacemaking and toward learning conflict-resolving skills.

Have you ever watched little kids when their parents fight? They desperately hold their ears. That means kids crave calm and quiet. So we can easily teach a child that peace is the way.

Enlist Professional Help

If you can't do that by yourself, ask for help. Leading our kids is easy when they are guidable, but hard when they have strong personalities. Or if we've been coasting as parents for some time, then suddenly realize we need to pull in the reins—that's difficult. But it is necessary when our kids have gotten out of control.

Indeed, laissez-faire childrearing attitudes can have terrible consequences not only for our own sons or daughters, who may hurt themselves with a gun or other weapon, but also for whole communities.

But we can take charge and must.

If our own efforts to disinterest kids in guns don't seem to help, we can't sit back any more hoping that Crystal and Kevin will outgrow their love for fire, their passion for guns, their wooing of weaponry. We must seek help. Start with a school staff member and insist on referrals to counselors, child psychologists, psychiatrists, or other medical personnel. All kids can be directed away from their harmful attachments. It's up to the parent to take steps to see that it's done. Teachers also must disenchant their students with weaponry. The Resource Guide on page 185 lists Web sites and groups that will help, if only we take that first step.

Lobby for "Good" Guns

For all those of us with guns, we need new guns—those that have the most sophisticated locking mechanisms available. Several of those GOOD guns, which is my term and stands for Guaranteed Only-Owner Design, are now in the process of being perfected. (As this book went to press, various versions of them were not on the market yet.) But what a blessing it will be to have guns that work only via fingerprint or another identifying mark of the owner. Therefore, in the future, "good" guns could be used only for the purpose they were meant—for owners to protect themselves from danger. For safety and security reasons and of course for the defense of our nation.

Indeed, guns were never meant to end up in the hands of criminals, torturers, bandits, thieves, and gangsters of all kinds. Or in the hands of oppressors, extortionists, kidnappers, and men and women who want to subdue others and deny them their rights.

Or in the hands of our kids.

So what we need now is to switch to guns with mechanisms that are inoperable in any hand except the rightful owner's. These new "good" guns will give us back confidence in our weapons, which will again become tools only for law enforcement, for personal protection, as military equipment, or part of the hunting experience.

With "good" guns, fathers will still be able to pass on their outdoor skills to their sons and daughters. Men and women will still be able to protect themselves against crime, and in the case of war, against the enemy. But no longer will all of us have to live daily in fear of our lives.

Crime also will abate. Sure, criminals will not reduce their unlawful activities just because of the existence of "good" guns—that is, guns that aren't accessible to them since gun salesmen won't be able to sell them to people convicted of crimes or to underage people or to unstable folks. But certainly the quick-draw mentality will disappear. Without more and more guns of the old, unsecured type in the hands of the bad guys, less damage will be inflicted upon their victims. And finally the ever-increasing crime statistics will become more in line with those of countries that have strict gun control.

Naturally the process to switch from the old guns, which must become outdated, bought back, and destroyed, to the new "good" guns will take a few years. But with the support of the whole country, this process can take place. Why not implement the latest technological advances we have into all weaponry?

Why not work for stricter gun control laws in the process?

And most important, why not forever keep guns out of the hands of our babies?

Sign 4: Alienation at School

A quick and easy way to assess our kids' violence-proneness is to measure their interest in school. That can be done in mere minutes. Just take a close look at their most recent report cards. Apathy toward academics is a definite red flag.

School is a vital component in kids' lives. Kids are young human beings who are acquiring knowledge. They're sponges looking to absorb new learning.

But when the pathway to new learning is obstructed, kids are denied their role as students. Then they have no purpose; their mental growth has been thwarted, and there is nothing else for them to do. They're like plants straining to grow straight and tall, yet have no room. Their development is stunted. In nature, that may produce gnarled tree trunks. In children, it produces explosive feelings that can lead to violence.

Thus, kids without any means to grow academically are frequently on the verge of aggression. There's no doubt that a close feeling toward school, which expresses itself in either doing well scholastically or at least in wanting to do well, is key. For that reason, the kid-school connection is critical. If it's not working, there's trouble ahead. The good news, however, is that of all the warning signs of violence among kids, this one is the easiest to take care of.

Disinterest in Grades

How many people go to work every day and don't care about a paycheck? Very few. And how many wouldn't note a drop in their salary and be concerned about that? Even fewer.

The same is true for kids. To them school is as important as work to adults. That's their job. Therefore, a low grade or failing a test must be of utmost importance to them—or should be. It's a sign that not all is well when Crystal isn't doing all she can, or doesn't care about her school performance.

Similarly, a child who shows little interest in doing schoolwork or homework or studying is telling us something—that is, I need help. Not participating in school-assigned work and a disinterest in studies in general, and in school skills in particular, will always result in low grades. And when kids seem satisfied in making C's, D's, and F's, we must pay close attention.

Of course, an occasional poor grade is normal. But the reaction the youngster has to this rare occurrence is telling. If the child is upset over a low grade and it stirs him on to intensifying his efforts, all is well. But if the child acts nonchalant when low marks keep reappearing, we must wake up. That includes parents and teachers.

It's not just the bad grades, but the simple fact that kids shrug them off when they bring in below-average results that must alarm us. That's an omen that the youngster is getting estranged from what should matter to him most. And an estrangement from an environment in which one spends so much time is always a bad sign. That can lead to worse school difficulties. In fact, it can lead to outbursts of serious negative behaviors.

Attendance Problems

Another sign of trouble is a child's attendance pattern. Of course, not every child has robust health and can avoid all childhood illnesses. Some kids can't have perfect attendance, no matter how hard they try. They have allergies or twist their ankle—whatever the case may be. It's their attitude toward their school attendance that counts, not how many days they have actually missed. If a child is eager to return to class even with sniffles or the remnants of flu, all is well, no matter how many days in the school year she has missed.

However, an entirely different scenario occurs with the youngster who seeks any excuse to stay home. In the early grades, school phobia—that is, a child actually fears going to school—can be a problem. This can be treated with the help of school counselors, and is not a sign of increased violence-proneness.

But many students get in the habit of staying home for no reason other than "not feeling like going to school." Our kids' feeling that way isn't unfounded. Often boys who aren't good athletes come up with that excuse on days they have physical education, girls have test anxiety, and vice versa. Nevertheless, this must be handled early on. Once a student gets away with staying home just because she feels like it, she will only repeat that pattern. In years to come, when a parent tries to put a stop to the skipping habit, Crystal will pretend to go to school, then duck out of the building or leave with her friends after home-room, once they've been counted present.

Many kids also hide out in bathrooms or take three lunch periods or "study" in the library for hours without ever going to class. Some students manage to fool their parents this way for days or weeks. By then they have fallen so far behind in their work and are ashamed to face the teacher that they truly have good reasons for staying home. Those reasons range from feeling depressed to having stomachaches, to self-induced ill-nesses like deliberate sports injuries or poisoning due to eating food or substances they know are bad. Anything to get out of school!

An occasional day off from school for a high-achieving youngster can actually be beneficial, if the parent keeps the child out for good reasons or a special reward, a trip, or a visit to relatives. But what must worry us is the child who falls into the habit of conjuring up all kinds of pains just so she doesn't have to go to school. Such a child will rarely stay in bed once allowed to stay home. Most likely her day at home will be spent doing things that aren't productive, such as watching forbidden TV shows or visiting off-limits Internet sites.

It's for that reason that, when a child refuses to go to school, she should be forced to stay in bed all day, after a visit to the doctor, of course. Additionally, parents should find out if the friends of their kids are staying out too. Curiosity is key here. It's always a bad sign if best friends are absent the same day. Teachers must realize that as well.

Kids who habitually play hooky deepen their feeling of alien-ation from school. For every day out, most kids need several days to catch up. So skipping is a serious matter and should be dealt with immediately, since it can lead to falling scores, not just in quiz grades, but in achievement tests. That's where serious problems arise.

Falling Scores

To assess the degree of a youngster's increasing alienation, report cards should be compared each time new ones are issued. Look for a steady learning level or an improvement in grades over the course of the year. Of course, minor dips may occur. But any time there's a drastic descent, parents must step in. When youngsters who previously made the honor roll suddenly bring home grades that are more than one level lower than before— that is, where they used to make A's, they now make C's or D's— parents must realize there's a problem. First, of course, the child should be asked for an explanation. Then the parent must investigate further what's going on in school.

Think back to when your baby first started walking and learned to walk well. Wouldn't a sudden refusal to walk or a regression back to crawling have concerned you? You bet. The same is true for school and kids. Any reverting back to lower achievement must alert us.

This starts in child care. Any time a child's mental growth becomes stunted, teachers must notice it. They must learn to think outside their weekly units or instructional tasks and develop an overview of their students.

A good score early in the academic year will tell them that the student has the basic understanding of the subject. And another good or even higher grade is to be expected as the school year goes on. But at no time should a sudden drop in scores be overlooked, because it can only mean one of two things:

1. The student isn't absorbing new information. (That is a stumbling block that needs attention before it becomes a permanent roadblock that will alienate Crystal from school forever.) Or,

2. The student has stopped caring about the subject, in which case she has built up an impediment to skill growth herself. That will not disappear on its own. If left undealt with, it may even estrange a student further from a formerly close school environment until she lashes out at school, classmates, and teachers in a violent way. Indeed, most school shooters felt alienated from their school long before they committed their tragic acts.

Schools and kids should go hand in hand, so let's reunite them.

Success Strategies

Evaluate School Skills and Health

The first step is to have your child's basic skills evaluated. That's best done by an outside professional, such as an educational testing facility. Often kids pretend to be good readers, while in reality they're only excellent listeners. Other kids are so smart they can absorb all kinds of difficult material just by paying attention in class.

But they can't read the chalkboard or don't process the information the same way their classmates do. They may be dyslexic, need glasses, or have any number of other learning challenges. Nevertheless, they're bright or even brighter than the other kids in class. But the fact that they're learning differently soon begins to affect them, especially as they move up through the grades.

In fact, many youngsters who do well in elementary school but start making low grades in middle school fall into this category and must be tested. Of course, ADD (Attention Deficit Disorder) students belong to this group, but fortunately now there are new treatments available, not just drugs.

Whatever the diagnosis may be, parents must act on it, for kids can only be reconnected to their school environment if the underlying causes for their school dysfunction are found and treated. And teachers, you are usually the first to spot any emerging school alienation. So please notify parents at once. Mom and Dad can't get to work on the problem if they don't know about it.

Increase School Interest

This is simple: You help your child become more interested in school. You do that by making connections between school and Kevin. Therefore, once his reading and writing skills are up to par (and if they're not, get him the help he needs), you scout for books and other materials geared to his special interests. Start by throwing out all kinds of topics, from aviary to zoology. If he perks up at any of those topics, make a note of it, call your favorite bookstore and have them pull up lists of books dealing with the subject. That's it.

But often students have fallen by the wayside in earlier grades, so their reading comprehension skills, for example, are not what they should be. Thus, teachers and parents must track down materials on the child's reading level, not their actual grade level. These materials must never be insulting or babyish to the youngster. An eighth-grader is embarrassed having to read Dr. Seuss books unless he is entertaining a group of first graders or is studying *The Cat in the Hat* as a model, so he can write a book of rhyme himself.

Fortunately, a host of high-interest materials for low-skill readers exists. Also, methods of bringing a slow reader or a slow math student back into the fold are available in most schools. Kids enjoy a school environment where they can shine. Success brings more success, so interest in school is always furthered by increasing one's children's abilities in school.

The truth is, when students make A's and B's, their participation in scholastic matters grows. It's kids with average or low grades who easily lose interest in their academics, since they have been robbed of the opportunity to excel. Thus, heightened interest often depends on increasing basic skills, on continued practice, and on enrolling kids in classes or programs where they can succeed.

And in preschool and grade school, it's all low-scoring kids we must watch now, not just the one group directly in our care. So teachers and caregivers, please network and trade timely teaching tips.

Highlight Talents

A wonderful way to help kids enjoy school more is to create a tie between a child's natural talents and school activities. Kids will not want to be absent from any course they love. If, for example, a youngster is good in music, the parent should make sure he is enrolled in a music class, either choir or band, in school.

The same goes for art, drama, or an athletic talent. If a child is good at sports, getting her into a school sports team is of the utmost importance. Kids who participate in volleyball and have a chance to show their stuff in the gym or on the court always have a better outlook on school. Frequently they maintain higher grades too, not only because their coach requires certain grade point averages, but also because many of their athletic peers are go-getters who have college aspirations. That attitude of ambition rubs off.

Also, the more fun activities kids engage in in school, the better they do in other school subjects. It's as if putting out their best efforts in one area stimulates them in other areas. Many athletes make excellent grades.

That also goes for students' talents other areas, whether in leadership or in academic skills. Often kids who want to run for student office must meet high academic standards as well. So if Crystal shows a leaning toward that, help her with her posters and speeches. Or if Kevin likes to debate, practice with him and ask his teachers for extra help.

And those kids who have a flair for writing, math, or science should be encouraged to take part in whatever special programs exist in their schools—from the school magazine to the yearbook, from the math club to the science fair. Each time a youngster has an opportunity to explore her extra talents, she feels closer to school, thus getting immunized against resorting to school violence. We don't destroy what we cherish; we don't kill what we love. We honor what's dear in our hearts.

We don't hurt it or blow it away.

Shore Up Attendance

Even the most talented kids will lose out if they're absent from school too often. Many academic programs demand tons of catch-up work for each day the student is out, so it's extremely important for kids not to miss school.

Of course, in the case of an illness, nothing can be done except to try to keep the students caught up via e-mail. And supervision of the completed assignments is key. Daily work completed should be forwarded to the teachers who made the assignments. While that is a makeshift approach to getting caught up, it's better than nothing.

To make sure your child is not skipping, parents should mark on their calendar any day their child has a legitimate reason for staying home. Then when report cards come out and denote seven absences, a parent has an easy way to check if their child has been skipping. Older kids often leave for school, then skip classes. That behavior must be stopped just as soon as it rears its head.

An interest in having perfect or near-perfect attendance should be cultivated in the child early on. That's done by example; parents should never brag about their own work-ditching or blowing-off-school exploits. And teachers should never raise an eyebrow when a well-known skipper returns to class and say, "Kevin, how nice of you to drop in!" All the teacher needs to do is smile and make all students feel included. We must value every teachable moment and mold the minds of all our kids, no matter how unteachable they appear to be. Indeed, every kid is in need of a lesson—the lesson of love, at least, if no other.

Some kids need that lesson several times, but no kid is a hopeless case. Only adults are hopeless, if they give up.

Provide Tutoring

One challenge is that our kids' grasps on school concepts grow at different speeds. No two students ever learn at the same rate. So parents, even if your older children breezed right through Algebra II or Spanish IV, when a child in the family has trouble with a subject, a solution must be found. It's never a good idea just to accept a kid's failure in a course or at a particular grade level, since all subjects build on previous ones. Third-grade skills are important for fourth grade.

Thus, when a student has to struggle with his regular assignments and his grades hover at the failing point, parents should step in. First the teacher should be asked for advice. Maybe the student isn't trying hard enough, is sitting too far away from the chalkboard, is too absorbed with friends, or is not paying attention. A new seating arrangement should be tried, then perhaps another class. Often a student will do better when removed from a non-studious bunch. Also more homework time must be set aside each evening and studying for tests must be taken seriously.

But if the youngster still has a hard time, hiring a tutor may be the correct move. Some tutors are college kids who can break down school concepts into smaller bites so a child can gobble them up better. Also the emphasis placed on learning, which becomes evident through the appearance of a weekly tutor, can make the child shift his attention to the task at hand.

Many schools have lists of potential tutors. Or checking with other parents may provide names of suitable instructors. In some cases retired teachers have the patience that's needed to get the lesson across to a youngster who has a hard time. We should avail ourselves to the incredible sources of excellence that experienced teachers provide.

Lean on Learning Centers

These days learning centers have sprung up in many communities, especially in larger cities. There, for a fee, Crystal is tested, then introduced to the latest materials that will help her advance.

What's beneficial in this approach is that she will meet other kids who are also trying to improve their grades. Thus, striving students will find they're not alone. And studying in a small group is more fun for some kids than working alone. Also, many up-to-date learning centers are chockfull of electronic study games. Computer lessons can be especially fun for a child who is "bored" with books. Plus, hints and other suggestions obtained at a learning center will set parents on the right path to adding software to their home computers. Then students can practice what they learn at the center, which in turn will give them the cutting edge in the classroom.

Furthermore, the same centers or different ones can be an important resource later, when kids enter high school and face college preparatory tests and deadlines. They are also a boon to child care workers and teachers, for they use efficient methods to further education. Young teachers should visit all the learning centers they can and become shameless copycats—not of materials, of course, but of all masterful methods.

For don't we all want the same thing—to help our kids know more? And the thrilling thing about teachers is that they're learners themselves. And there's always more to learn.

Provide Early College Exposure

Extra-smart kids, especially, often get disenchanted with the middle and high school routine. For them, it's nothing but the "same old, same old," the same stories told in books and lessons that they have heard so many times before. Since elementary and middle schools are now trying to upgrade their instruction, much material that formerly wasn't covered until high school is now introduced in the early grades. Thus, high schoolers are often placed on "hold," and don't experience new material and skills. They can already write a decent three-page essay, have enough math and foreign language skills to feel confident, know basic science concepts, and enough about cyberspace so they can easily access more information if they so desire.

For the youngster who doesn't have the "stick-to-it" skills of a truly serious student but is very bright, a certain restlessness sets in. While Crystal isn't making all A's and never will, she is still savvy enough to breeze through high school without having to study much. And if this trend continues, she becomes easily anti-intellectual. That is, she develops an anti-school attitude because her academic needs aren't met.

In most schools, the geniuses and the gutter kids get the most attention. Those in between tend to be overlooked. So students who seem bright but bored should be allowed to take one class with truly serious students, so they will get a wake-up call. Enroll them in an early college admission program or some other accelerated program that gives college credit in high school. Often the bored high schooler gets too blasé for her own good. In the company of really bright and older but dedicated college students, she wakes up and realizes that there is a world of learning yet to be conquered.

Divide and Conquer

A different approach must be found for the student who is alienated from school because he just can't keep up, despite tutoring and after-school work at a learning center.

In that case, a divide-and-conquer tactic has to be employed. Not every student can successfully master all subjects at the same time and frankly, some students just aren't good in academics. But all of them can pass their grade level.

When failure has occurred in more than one subject, it's best to split up the problem and attack one difficult subject at a time. Usually the underlying reason is a lack of reading ability and comprehension.

One reason for some students' low reading and language development is the increase in divorce. If divorce occurs while the children are in the process of learning basic reading skills, their academic development can be delayed. That happens frequently with boys. It's not that they suffer more from divorce than girls, but some of them are less verbal to begin with. Girls recover faster than boys from a drop in language skills caused by the trauma of divorce.

But no matter what the cause, we must always begin with that basic skill. If reading scores are substantially below grade level, that issue must be addressed first. In so many cases, poor readers develop excellent listening skills, have terrific memories, and are great actors. For a number of years they can bluff their way through school. But sooner or later, their deficient reading skills surface.

So be glad if it turns out that your youngster's only behind in his reading skills, then get to work on the problem. Enlist the guidance counselor or principal. Often a student's school schedule can be modified to make sure he has several classes a day in reading and language until he is caught up again. Only after the underlying problem of below-par reading and comprehension is dealt with, however, can the other failing classes or subjects be tackled successfully.

Check Out Summer School

Summer can be an excellent time in which kids whose school skills are in arrears can make progress. Of course, not all of summer should be devoted to catching up on scholastics, but at least half the time ought to be devoted to rigorous schoolwork. Often the school the student attends has a summer school program, or maybe another school in the area has one.

Again, begin with the child's teacher and ask for suggestions. Sometimes private schools, charter schools, or parochial schools offer the best summer programs for a youngster who has lost faith in herself academically. What is good about sending Crystal to a summer school she doesn't regularly attend is that she begins with a clean slate. So no more will a series of failed papers and undone assignments hang over her head like Damocles' sword.

Also the vicious cycle of several kids failing together can be broken if your unsuccessful child takes a course in unfamiliar surroundings. Kids often bond with less capable ones out of a need to be tops with somebody. So swiftly removing the downward drag of children who are even less capable in their academic subjects is a boon. Also, a new teacher may have a new take on how to best reach and teach a child who is on the verge of falling behind.

And all schools should get the word out as to their make-up

programs. Never ever should a failing child be flung to the winds. "We will work wonders with all kids," should be the motto of all teachers.

Investigate Academic Camps

Academic camps can also help. They run the gamut from science camps to creative writing programs. Many last from two to four weeks and often have other components, such as sports programs or time slots for artistic expression. It's best to explain the strong points of the various summer camps to Kevin, then let him choose. Kids really want to be comfortable in their regular classes, and explaining to Kevin, not blaming him, that he is a year behind in school skills will get him to cooperate. If the child has input into the camp selection, the benefits from the program can be doubled or tripled.

Ask your youngster what interests him. If it's water sports, sailing, canoeing, search for a camp that combines the emphasis on the academic skill that needs boosting with the sports or other leisure activity the child likes. The Internet is your ally in this quest.

Or—and this can really work—immerse the child totally in a camp that does nothing but push the one skill he has trouble with. Often a one-time total immersion in just one subject can bring the same result that several partial visits or short programs might.

For example, a youngster who resists reading can be sent to a Great Books for Kids camp. There everyone reads as many books a week as possible, and authors of children's literature are speakers. Kids research the lives of those authors, write their book reports, and e-mail them home to you so you can keep up with their progress.

That's key—keeping up with the progress kids make as they begin to catch up on their school skills, thus closing the gap between them and school.

Get Personally Involved

Our children watch what fascinates us. When they see us absorbed in things, they get infected by the same bug. So when we involve ourselves in the daily affairs of their school and give them our best efforts, our efforts become contagious. Our children wonder: What makes Mom and Dad so excited about running for PTA office? Heading up that committee to beautify the school grounds? Raising money for new band uniforms?

And if we start this process early, our kids grow up considering our school participation a normal part of their lives. Thus, they too will delve into school projects, which will be an antidote to any school alienation. The school will be their buddy.

But even if we don't dive into school-related organizations or sign up for committees until later in our kids' academic careers, whatever attempts we make to communicate positively with the school environment will have major benefits. Kids who see their folks immersed in school issues, serving on the attendance committee or the yearly school calendar group, or who join in setting up SAT study programs or who contribute financially to new trophy cases in the lobby or to an alcohol-free after-graduation party, can't help but at least be drawn into the ensuing discussions about those efforts.

Therefore, they too become more closely attached to their school. You can't hate or be withdrawn from something you know inside out. And when kids know more about the behind-the-scenes workings of their school, they care more. Their grades seem more meaningful and start rising.

Enthusiastic teachers will also engage their kids. So please, pull your pupils in with powerful projects and lesson plans. No one can attach them better to academics than you!

Review Progress Constantly

If a child who has been lagging begins to respond, he needs to be watched closely. He can too easily fall back into a lack of caring about schoolwork or into an attitude of not trying. Catching up on school skills is hard. For that reason, it's not enough for the parent of a school-challenged child to wait until report cards come out, as would be common practice with a child whose skills measure up. If you have a youngster who has to struggle to keep up or is in the process of pulling up her grades, check with her teachers every couple of weeks. You don't want the child to get too far behind again.

Of course, the tendency might be to check every day or send a note to the teacher every other day, but that's too strict. Kids don't like to be singled out for their school failings or suspected low grades. So, checking in with the teacher in private every two weeks is sufficient, as well as looking at the papers the child brings home.

Yet at no time should parents relax totally once the first good report card comes home and think that the problem's been solved. School skills must be watched like diets. Once you've lost the unwanted weight you can't go back to a high-fat, high-calorie constant pigging out, can you?

Same goes for kids. Once they have changed for the better, have started studying, and know how to study, the process of reviewing their progress must go on. It only ends when Crystal has graduated from high school and is enrolled in college. Even then it helps to keep up with her classes.

At no time should kids who have been alienated from their school due to poor grades or attendance problems be suddenly abandoned at age eleven, twelve, or thirteen. This happens earlier and earlier these days. Parents assume it's the duty of the schools to take over most of the child development. Schools claim it's the duty of the parents to rear their children. So both groups point at each other and delegate their responsibilities.

They're *all* America's kids. And to keep them from turning to violence, supervision is key. Too much supervision is preferred to too little, even in case where no flags indicate violence-prone behavior.

To keep our kids safe, we must not only arm ourselves with knowledge of the factors that make them violent and make sure our own offspring don't develop those signs, but we must also teach our violence-proofed youngsters to be on the lookout for other kids who haven't gone through the process of becoming safe kids.

We must constantly engage in so much violence-proofing activity that not one single kid is left out. Not one.

Sign 5: Negative Friendships

Countless proverbs and adages point to this warning sign, such as, "Birds of a feather flock together," or, "Who lies down with dogs gets up with fleas," or, "Show me your friends and I show you who you are...."

Indeed, the friends our kids cultivate are a good indication of who they will become, if they aren't already so inclined. So we must closely observe the youngsters our kids associate with. From early on in school, kids begin to transfer their allegiance away from their parents and onto their peer groups.

While this process usually takes a few years, from fifth or sixth grade on it only strengthens. Often by the end of middle school or the beginning of high school, kids relate to one another almost as heavily or more than they do to their parents. And in high school the peer influence truly rears its head. Many students of that age prefer the company of their age group and banish their parents to the back burners, especially if those parents have been a weak influence to begin with.

It's at this age that kids don't want to be seen shopping with their parents at the mall. The majority of teenagers will still accept their parents' presence in the background, but that doesn't mean they don't need it. As a matter of fact, the more teens shove their parents out of the way, the more they need their moms' and dads' guidance, not in a hovering manner but in a behind-the-scene, supportive way.

Growing up means learning to stand on one's own feet. It means letting go of Mom's hand, then clutching the hand of a peer before standing totally alone.

It's that in-between process of overrelating to one's age group that can cause problems. Since kids do not have good judgment about their peer groups, they frequently make bad choices. As a matter of fact, choosing "positive" friends, that is, friends who will aid in a child's healthy inner and outer growth, is a difficult skill that must be taught.

Yet it can't be taught outright, the way we teach kids how to drive a car or to be safe with guns. The way to find the right friends has to be taught indirectly. But it's one of the most important lessons kids must learn, since negative friendships can be extremely detrimental.

Indeed, if our children pick pals who drag them down in the gutter, the effect is just as bad as if they were the originators of the negative behavior themselves. It doesn't matter if our kids think of an act of vandalism or violence themselves or if they are persuaded to join in by their peers. The end result is always the same: Windows smashed in a new house, car tires slashed for the fun of it, mailboxes blown up with pipe bombs, a school that's been torched, a store broken into, a homeless man set on fire, a small child attacked, a classmate killed in a demon ritual, a twelve-year-old girl or boy raped, classmates and teachers blown away. All these acts are destructive, whether they originate first in your daughter's head or in those of her friends who convince her to participate.

We must recognize that the more violence-prone our kids' friends are, the more violence-prone our children will be. Not only does their friends' antisocial behavior rub off on them, but their combined brightness and creativity turned sinister will escalate a little prank into truly criminal activity. Soon what an individual borderline violent kid could have thought up by himself is eclipsed by the teen pack or gang mentality that always tries to top any previous highjinks.

Just as the will to do good is expanded when kids who're positioned to do good brainstorm, so is the potential for harm explosively enlarged by peers who are a bad influence. One off-the-cuff remark about what one would like to do to a classmate or teacher soon sparks a deep discussion on how much harm can be done (and when).

And it's the kids' inability to stop this avalanche of negative peer pressure, once a sinister idea has been born, that is the problem. Alone, a teen may have wishes of revenge or daydreams of getting back at somebody, at a bully or at someone from another ethnic group, but in a group, the only-dreamed-about crime takes on a life of its own.

Then a tiny idea mushrooms. Indeed, its continued feeding keeps the group or gang together. Soon the negative friends meet only to advance their plotting and antisocial plans. Before long, it's a matter of losing face, that is, losing the support of one's peers, that stops a kid from leaving this cycle of hate-mongering and bad deed-planning. Very few kids have the strength at that point to say no.

For by then other embarrassing acts have taken place, and a blackmail scheme is in force. How can good kids stop participating in something wrong if they're already up to their necks in the planning or in smaller, earlier misdeeds?

Therefore, we must examine very carefully the kids our offspring choose to spend time with. And as teachers we must watch out for all borderline kids. The least harmful of these are the "weird" dressers.

"Weird" Appearance

Fortunately, weird dressers are easy to spot. Just look at what the kids your children spend time with are wearing. But, please, don't start screaming about how awful young kids look today. If you're unsure, because kids' attire has changed drastically over the past thirty years, do the following: Observe the "weird" kids, make a mental note of what they're wearing, then go for a comparison check to your kid's school.

There you'll see what all the other kids wear nowadays. Surely you don't want Crystal to be the only girl dressed in round-collared pastel blouses, pleated skirts, and white socks with ruffles and Mary Janes, when every other girl in class is decked out in thick-soled sneakers, blue jeans, and loose sweaters. So just aim for the middle ground in the clothes you buy for your child and what you hope your child's friends will wear. Always have a flexible approach. Clothes and even hairstyles are a fairly harmless way for kids to test their mettle, to show their growing independence, or let out healthy stirrings of rebellion. As long as their school dress codes aren't violated and decency prevails, don't be too harsh in criticizing your kids' friends.

A totally outlandish appearance, however, ought to give you pause. These days all our kids have all kinds of clothing options. So they should look reasonably acceptable. If your son's or daughter's friends are the most outrageously dressed kids in school, then it's time to worry. And if their hair is neon blue and their lipstick matches; if even boys wear makeup and numerous chains and metal studs on jackets, emulating the biker look; if they seem to dress only to enrage and engage the adult world in an argument, then their weird clothing is more than trying to find their own style or breaking away from the frumpy appearance of their folks.

Numerous recent articles in popular magazines like *Newsweek* agree: We should be concerned by kids who dress as a way to get back at the "enemy," who want to smack adults in the face by exposing body parts that ought to be covered, who flaunt their underwear as outerwear, and who believe the more ragged, bedraggled, grimy, grungy, and seedy they can appear, the more satisfaction they get. All kids who're determined to kick the adult world in the shins every day by their disgusting looks need to be watched. And worried over.

Your child doesn't need "friends" like that.

Also, please, read what's on their T-shirts. If it's sports logos or school mottoes, fine. If it's curse words, violent phrases, obscure references to drugs, guns, sex, gangs, or death, those T-shirts are not acceptable. Even if your child doesn't wear such a shirt, he absorbs the message every time he's around the offensive T-shirt wearers. And you don't want your youngster exposed to constant hate messages. They will imprint themselves on the mind of your child and in his heart. And our children's hearts are the most precious things there are. Hate has no place in them.

Teachers also need to observe what kids wear. To avoid problems, a simple dress code that upholds basic decency standards must be established in every child care and educational institution.

Smoking, Drugs, Alcohol, and Sex

The next step up in harmful peer groups are those kids who lead our youngsters to smoking, drugs, alcohol, and sex. The following numbers show how just many kids get misled every day. According to Teen Help Adolescent Resources (see the Resource Guide, page 185), in the next twenty-four hours, 2,795 teenage girls will become pregnant, and 15,006 teens will use drugs for the first time.

The dangers of kids being influenced the wrong way by their peers are real. In any clique, the lowest common human denominator always prevails. So if the "friends" enjoy random vandalism, for example, your child is likely to pick up that habit whether you know it or not. It's never a question of whether your offspring will pick up the toxic behavior, it's only a question of when. Sure, some kids can withstand harmful peer pressure for a short time and others a little longer. But no youngster can do so indefinitely, because that would exclude her from the group forever.

And that's one thing your kid doesn't want—exclusion from a group of close friends.

So step in before it's too late, and always know that a bad clique that spends many hours together will commit many crimes together. So if anyone among your kids' friends drinks, they all will, sooner or later. And if anyone in the group smokes cigarettes, it's a sure thing all will smoke. Then, of course, they graduate to marijuana and other drugs. With kids, the "growth process" for getting into trouble is always forward and is always a dangerous step up. And never backward to lesser infractions.

Once they have started drinking and doing drugs, there's nothing left but sex, and that in the most negative of forms.

With kids prone to violence, it will probably include force and pain. And again, whatever harm those practices cause can never be undone. It only worsens by degrees.

Bad kids go from bad to worse to worst. Do you want your most precious gift, your child, involved in that? Of course not. So watch out for the smell of alcohol or cigarettes or marijuana when your offspring and their friends congregate at your house. Even the slightest hint of their participating in those three should raise a red flag immediately. Teachers, in your classrooms, don't cancel your sense of smell. If you get a whiff of anything that worries you, please, investigate.

If you don't, who will?

Self-Mutilation

The most serious negative behavior that your child's friends can exhibit is self-mutilation. Self-mutilation deals with hurting oneself and is often only a few steps away from hurting others. These days some kids have so much inner pain that they use outer pain to express themselves. They don't care whether they inflict it on themselves or others. Or whether they turn into murderers or turn their friends into murderers.

The process of self-mutilating may begin with radical haircuts, shaved heads, violent tattoos all over, bold pictures and hate messages permanently etched into the skin. Even troubled kids in first or second grade may scratch initials or slogans on their forearms, then go over them in ink so many times that their skin scars permanently. Then they advance to piercing every body part that can be pierced, from merely unusual places such as eyebrows, tips of noses, and tongues to nipples, navels, and other parts below the belt.

So if your kid's friends have much more than pierced ear-lobes, watch out. An overabundance of pierced body parts bespeaks of what's inside the child. There are kids who derive pleasure from the uncomfortable presence of metal stuck through the most sensitive parts of their bodies, and you do not want your child around kids who don't have normal pain meters.

Kids who either enjoy pain or can't feel it will also enjoy inflicting pain. Therefore, be wary of any friend your child brings home who looks like a sewing kit exploded in his face. Of course, you may think you can help your child's friends by showing them the folly of such behavior. You want to love their pains away. But what often happens is that your child thinks you're condoning all that piercing. Then Kevin will follow suit, except he will take it a step further. Naturally, you never want to turn your back on any kid in pain, but first concentrate on Kevin.

As we said earlier, kids' negative behavior is like an avalanche: Once it's set into motion, it's hard to stop. So don't wait until Kevin has become closely enmeshed with kids whose appearance gives you the creeps. Head off troubles early on with the following simple techniques.

Success Strategies

Know Your Kids' Friends Well

Your first step is to meet your kids' friends. All of them. You do that by having an open-house policy and by proving with your actions that your children's friends are welcome to come over any time after school and on weekends. That is, so you can get a good look at them, observe them in their discussions, play, and watch them for violence-prone warning signs.

So, as soon as your kids make new friends, suggest they bring them home. If your kids are reluctant, spruce up the house or fix up the family room, until there's nothing your kids could be ashamed of. Teenagers especially have a low embarrassment threshold, but they're not generally shy in expressing what bothers them about their home and parents. So, if they suggest minor alterations around the house and yard, follow their advice. If they tell you to modernize too, do it.

Be alert, however, if your kids give excuses, such as the fact that they'd rather meet at their friend's house because that's "more convenient," or their friends have a pool and you don't, or basketball court or the latest tech toys. That's fine for a day or so. But continued refusal to bring friends home often means your kids are ashamed of the kinds of friends they have. Or that they've already begun to spend their free time with them in a manner you wouldn't like or with "hobbies" you'd be appalled to know about.

Carry out this test: Ask Kevin and Crystal when they'd like to have their friends over. If your kids give valid excuses why they don't—your place is too messy, there's nothing to do here—get to work on those within reason. Or suggest that you take them all to a pizza place or the lake. Then meet the friends, and be especially observant. From then on make it a habit to invite your child's pals for a cookout or some other treat a couple of times a month.

But if your children refuse to bring their friends home, get to the bottom of why. Start by getting the names of those friends and find out as much about them as possible. Do that at the next teacher conference. Just ask the teacher with whom your children spend their lunchtime, whom they sit with in the cafeteria, whom they talk to in class.

And if your suspicions turn out to be correct, and your kids' friends are a negative influence, go on to the next step.

Rescue Your Kids

Often kids, through no fault of their own, live in neighborhoods where there are no suitable playmates, attend a school that has a counterproductive culture, or are in classes with few positive peers. Then all your kids can do is form friendships with the wrong crowd. Sometimes it's a small slip from early on—maybe Kevin made a low grade or Crystal got sent to the office once for as small infraction—and then your kids are forever enrolled in the troublemaker club, that is, in the group of kids that thrives on mischief in school, which escalates to minor malfunctioning in society, then mushrooms into major mayhem.

So break the vicious cycle. Immediately. You have to snatch your child out of the clutches of perilous peers. Believe me, that's not easy. No matter how you try to steer your offspring toward better behaved kids or more positive friendships, if Kevin remains in a class of clowns whose rowdiness continues to grow, he will not break away. There isn't a parent strong enough to come between a teen and his peers if they have already bonded.

Of course, you first ask for help from the teacher. Always start with that. Early on, having Crystal sit somewhere else in the classroom and away from the talkers can be beneficial. Also having her move to another class helps. That often brings about a different lunch schedule, which can sever the cohesion that is developing between her and the nonstudents.

But if that's no help, more drastic steps must be taken.

Introduce Kids to Positive Friends

The good news is that just as kids relate closely with the wrong group of friends, so do they with the right group—other kids who are doers, achievers, and on their way to becoming healthy and productive members of society.

The bad news is, how do you find such positive friends for your kids? And even if you track down one or two nice potential playmates, how can you shift your child's interest toward them and away from the much more alluring pals who do nothing but test the limits of school rules and society's standards?

Often the only thing to do is make a drastic change. If your child is enrolled in a school where the prevailing culture is anti-learning and pro-trouble, and when your child has already attached herself to a group that's inclined to do wrong, the only thing to do is to make a complete break. Move to another school district, which will provide a different school atmosphere.

But what if you love your present home? Ask yourself: What do you love more, your house or your own flesh and blood?

Even if the choice is hard, sometimes the only thing is to snatch your child from the clutches of a detrimental peer group, put her into a school and neighborhood that mesh with your values, and ensure that your child has many fabulous friends from whom to choose.

You must always put your actions where your priorities are. One woman in her forties moved back in with her mother so that she could afford to send her son to private school, away from bad influences.

Keep this in mind: You can always buy a dream house later. But can you get another dream son?

Educate Kids about Violence

Just making sure there are enough "good" kids in your neighborhood and in your child's school isn't enough, because all kids have the potential to stray. In today's society, dangers lurk everywhere for youngsters, even for the best-parented child.

So talking to Kevin and Crystal is key. Mention the dangers of smoking, drinking, doing drugs, and becoming sexually active at a young age, but do more than that. Make sure they have reading materials available, which you will read first, then have discussions on those topics. If possible, include your kids' friends in the talks. You want to be able to have your children and their buddies come to you with their concerns.

Also find out what programs exist in their school that will tackle the difficult problems—not only trigonometry or Latin III, but also how to get kids to abstain from drinking, smoking, doing drugs, and getting into sex prematurely. Often an active PTA will sponsor workshops for parents and teachers, and discussion groups for kids. So work with the school leadership and investigate what your PTA is doing to keep kids from becoming prey to these problems, which not only impede their progress but also encourage them to become violent.

Kids must be taught not only that doing something that's right is wonderful, but also that not doing something that's wrong is great. So often we train our kids to have good manners and to meet their deadlines in school and do their chores. Then we praise them afterward only for the good jobs they've done or their fine behavior. We don't praise them for not doing wrong.

Battle Their Shyness

One reason kids engage in smoking, drinking, drugs, and sex is that they're uncomfortable at parties, don't know how to say no, or feel like misfits if they don't plunge into those behaviors. So please, teach them to become more comfortable in social situations, which means you instruct them in overcoming shyness.

Like adults, kids can suffer from feelings of inferiority and shyness. Yet while grown-ups have learned to cope with feeling less than perfect, kids have not. To make a good impression, they will smoke anything that's offered, drink anything that's poured, and follow through with whatever action is suggested by an older boy, for instance.

That's why shyness must be counteracted from early on. We must teach kids that most people are shy. Shyness is a good thing and part of growth. Brashness and bravado are bad. So when kids feel shy at a gathering, when they hold back, become flustered or tongue-tied at social occasions, that only shows that they're growing inside. Everybody has those feelings at times. That's the way it's supposed to be. However, there are some kids who foolishly try to pretend they're not shy or insecure by acting like adults. By doing something dumb and getting into trouble.

So kids should be taught to spot those pretenders and learn not to be swayed in their own personal good conduct by brasher, more daring, or older kids. In school, students are often encouraged to write skits. What teachers must do now is give everyday, realistic topics that deal with subjects of real importance to our kids. Teachers should incorporate creative writing experiences that help kids to spot "big shot" kids who try to get others ensnared in harmful activities.

For example, English teachers from fifth grade up can say, "Write a one-act play in which a bad character tries to get another person to do something wrong. But don't make it too obvious. Then we'll present our skits and see if we can learn to spot the 'antagonist' in your skit and what methods he or she is trying to use." Most students love this type of "open-ended" writing assignment, and many discussions can ensue after the skits have been presented. The presentations themselves will remove some of the shyness kids have, plus this exercise emphasizes that the shy kid—not the one who gives in to every type of peer pressure, nor the one who does the enticing—is the true hero.

Indeed, all adults can teach our children to be less foolish and to remain strong in the face of negative influences. At home, practicing before a party can help our kids to assert themselves. "No, I don't want to," is all they need to learn. Teach your kids to say it: "No, I don't want to."

This phrase can be applied in any situation, and be amended as needed from year to year. If peer pressure to smoke sets in, Crystal can add, "I'll get kicked off the team." About drinking, she can say, "I hate the taste." To premature sex, she can say, "Not until I'm in college and only then if it's right."

And teachers, please, post this message in your school: "When it comes to books, say Yes. When it comes to peer pressure, just say No."

Teach De-stressing Skills

Like most adults, kids feel stress, in and out of school. So along with understanding shyness and learning how to deal with that, they need to learn how they can de-stress without being sucked into the dangerous DDSS (Drinking, Drugs, Smoking, and Sex) whirlpool. Healthy methods of getting rid of stress must be taught. They include exercise, focusing on upcoming events, and helping others. If Crystal learns how to amuse herself in a healthy manner, she will be less likely to latch on to negative friendships and habits.

Begin this de-stressing process by watching what Crystal does when she comes home from school after a particularly trying day. Does she flop on the couch? Watch a favorite program? Head outside for some fresh air? Call her girlfriends and rehash every detail of the "worst day in my whole entire life"?

Kids know instinctively what relaxes them, what relieves them, what renews them. All you do is make sure Kevin gets an extra helping of whatever it is that "chills" him out the most. Opening a youngster's eyes to new enjoyable activities and making his home life a place of calm and appreciation will help as well. Kids who are busy with positive leisure time pursuits rely less on their friends and more on themselves. Thus, the threat of undesirable kids is lessened.

But sometimes, no matter how hard you work at it, kids still flock only to those peers who are violence-prone. No matter where you move, they always seek out the worst youngsters on the block, kids who get into fights or come from backgrounds of abuse or from violent families, where parents drink or do drugs, or where kids are abused. This can happen when your own child has a soft heart and wants to save other, less fortunate youngsters. Unfortunately the young savior often becomes corrupted in the process, so you must step in.

Seek Professional Help

If Kevin always leans toward becoming friends with the most incorrigible kids around, you can spot that trend early. Child care workers have a special responsibility to point that out to parents. And by the time Kevin is in second or third grade, you can really see if he's hanging around only with hoodlums-in-the-making. Then, if after trying to separate him from those criminal elements, he's still only relating to them and has nothing but snide comments about the good kids in school, find out the real reason.

Often a child, through no reason we can discern, feels like an outsider. Or she may have been born with a gentle soul and be a dreamer, a missionary. Or, if there are several kids in the family, one may go against the grain, first as a lark, then seriously. So if Crystal only plays with the most precocious, most daring, most rebellious girls in class, and after you've exhausted all the steps outlined before and when at thirteen she looks and acts like a twenty-three-year-old, please seek help at once.

Begin at school, with her teachers and school counselor. Then seek out a child psychologist, but don't delay. By then Crystal may have been thinking of running away for a long time. Maybe she's even made a definite plan or has a much older group of friends who are influencing her ever more toward crime and violent behavior. In fact, kids who seek nothing but the worst-behaved kids around, whether they're bullies, skippers, or just bad influences, are asking for help. So you must get it for them, just like you'd get medical help for a child with a broken wrist that doesn't heal.

When it comes to your kid's friends, don't ever be negligent by just being glad your kids have somebody to play with. Give all your kid's friends a very careful look, and while you're at it, examine your own circle.

Change Your Own Circle of Friends

Some parents have friends who do nothing to enhance their own kids' chances for forming positive friendships. So maybe you need to widen your social circles. As in so many areas of life, kids learn by aping the behaviors of their parents. If you have friends who guzzle alcohol so much they pass out on your sofa, behave promiscuously, smoke marijuana, or talk about the many times they have gotten away with breaking the law, your kids will imitate that pattern of friend-making. Like it or not, while you have impressionable children at home, you have to curb your tendencies to associate only with your most unconventional friends from your college days. And, of course, when you yourself smoke, drink to excess, do drugs, or are unfaithful to your mate, what can you expect from your ten-year-old?

Your child is a miniature mirror image of you!

If liquor flows at your house and cocktails are part of the daily ritual, Crystal will absorb that lesson. But if your own good friends are productive members of the community who have a healthy outlook on life, your children will follow suit. They will learn to choose the kids of your productive friends as their friends or at least play with your friends' kids while they're visiting. And each time Kevin plays with a "good" kid, he will form a bond in the right direction. Each time Crystal joins other teens in some worthwhile activity, she learns not only how to make positive friends but also how to do good.

Model Healthy Solitude

What often makes kids so desperate to have friends, what makes them glom on to whatever peer group they can, good or bad, is the inability of youngsters to be their own best buddy. That means being able to spend time alone without getting bored. And that's definitely a lesson learned at home.

Ask yourself: What do I do with my free time? Do I spend some of it in quiet reflection or solitary pursuits? By our example, we need to instill in kids the ability to entertain themselves, the strength to find interesting things to do on their own, and the stick-to-it-iveness to follow through with enjoyable projects. And that means seeing you do it too. So get out your Cornwell or Grisham novel in the evening, sit quietly, and read it without any distractions. Or passionately work on your needlepoint or recipe collection and let your kids watch and help. You want Kevin to develop as many hour-filling interests he can. He does that by watching you.

Under no circumstances, however, make your children into isolated loners without friends, which happens when we cut off their old bad friends without giving them new good friends and providing them with what they want most: our closeness, leadership, and friendship.

Sign 6: Destructive Downtime

The sixth warning sign of violence-prone kids is how they spend their free time. The activities kids participate in are an outgrowth of their innermost values. If their values revolve only around themselves or if they are immature, tend to have a lazy streak, or are disinterested in physical activities, they can find themselves with too many unoccupied hours on their hands. And too many hours of nothing to do will result in nothing positive. Trust me. It will result in their finding something to do that's destructive. That can be downright deadly.

One reason is that kids these days have too much free time. No longer are lists of chores awaiting them when they come home. No longer do they work in family-owned businesses. Few kids nowadays have to drag out of bed at 5:00 A.M. and deliver newspapers. And most kids get an allowance, so why should they worry about work? Kids from divorced families are often plied with cash to make up for the absence of Father or Mother.

Indeed, many of today's kids are what used to be called spoiled. They have too much free time and everything they could ever want in material possessions. Parents often remember how hard their own growing-up years were, and that prompts them to go easy on their kids—too easy. Thus, parents now demand very little besides their kids' school attendance. Yet parents forget that schools have changed as well. The primary goal of many schools these days is to keep all kids enrolled until eighteen, and let academic standards fall by the wayside if they must.

In earlier generations schools prided themselves on kicking kids out who couldn't measure up academically. Now the opposite is true. School systems compete with one another in how many kids they can keep in, which of course demands a relaxation of scholastic standards.

Youngsters have less homework now. Kids are brighter, due to home computer use or maybe due to the "dumbing down" of school materials. So homework takes up less time than it used to.

Bright kids, in particular, can easily coast through school and earn B's and C's with minimal effort. This can lead to lots of downtime, which can result in an anti-work ethic or create an individual who always expects handouts.

Yes, our kids' downtime can turn into destructive time. And these days, destructive time does more than just cause our kids to meddle in mischief. It can lead to truly dire consequences.

Absence of Values

What lies at the root of kids' not knowing how to spend their free time constructively is the absence of values. In the past, kids learned their values not only from interaction with their parents but from churches and synagogues as well. Values were also taught in school by values-oriented literature, the study of great historical figures, the encouragement of service club participation, and the inclusion of homeroom periods where teachers had time to discuss current events or issues pertaining to school kids.

Nowadays, however, traditional sources of good values have either disappeared or have become suspect. Parents are too busy and kids don't go to religious meetings. In school, homeroom periods have fallen by the wayside. Kids' attendance is now taken on "bubble" sheets to be scanned in at the office. And teachers do not have time to "waste" talking about values.

In the larger culture, it's as if people with good value systems don't exist any more. Every day one reads in the media or sees on TV that people who you thought had strong value systems are really fakes, people who only pretended to be honorable. So whether it's in the church hierarchy, in government, or in the world of athletics, fewer and fewer people seem to possess real values.

That makes parents question their own values and leads to self-doubt. For if the top leadership in the country is crumbling on a personal level, how can the everyday citizen be expected to be filled with honor and teach his offspring to follow the highest ideals?

Yet, in times like ours, when hardly anyone with integrity seems to be around, true values are even more important than when they abound everywhere. Therefore, parents and teachers must make it a point to look for examples in modern life that teach good values. And they themselves must live their lives in such a manner that kids can absorb those high ideals by osmosis, if not through discussion and reminders.

Loner Lifestyle

What often interferes with that process, however, is the isolation that can engulf youngsters, which is caused by a number of factors. Certain kids have a hard time making friends. If they're shy or unpopular, they can withdraw into their own shells. And when they do have to face crowds, they're so desperate to fit in or become popular that they can find it difficult to avoid the slightest temptation. So whatever beginning good values they have fly out the window.

Also, smaller families are the norm today. No longer are children from their earliest days on exposed to crowds at home. Older brothers and sisters no longer share in the transmission of good values to younger siblings.

Moreover, the increased use of technology isolates kids. Just as their parents turn to cocooning, so some young kids learn early to spend a good deal of time with non-human companions—Beanie Babies, the TV, and their personal computer pal. All of those influences can come between kids and in-the-flesh friends. And inanimate objects do not transmit solid values.

Furthermore, some parents fear that potential friends will have a bad influence on their offspring. So, they embrace home-schooling to keep their kids as far away from outside influences as possible. Still others pack up their whole families and head for nature, reversing the trend of their forefathers who couldn't wait to move into town. Still other parents fear too much exposure to the errant-parent syndrome in their community. Thus, they overprotect their kids by keeping them isolated as much as possible. They'd like to insulate their kids with wads of cotton.

These attitudes can lead to a child's increased shyness and a feeling of peerlessness. In turn, this can brand a kid as a lonely figure who can't relate to others. Thus, Crystal is excluded from the everyday school interactions and has nothing but "boring" afternoons and evenings to look forward to. And a bored child, especially a smart bored child, can think up many unhealthy, unproductive, or even dangerous activities to occupy herself.

Work Ethic Void

Another cause for worry arises from the high living standard many families strive for these days. Both parents work, in often more than one job, just so their kids don't have to work at all and still can have as many Tommy Hilfiger shirts as the Jones' kids have. Or more.

Some parents want their kids not to work because they had to work as youngsters, and perhaps they didn't reach their own academic potential because they had to work. Or because they feel stymied in their jobs now, or their own careers are stunted. For those reasons, they want to make sure that their kids will go as far academically as possible. Whereas in the past most parents hoped their kids would finish high school, the bar has been raised. Now almost all parents want their kids to finish college. And yet an even tougher parental wish is emerging. These days many parents want their kids to go to graduate school to get a master's degree. In future generations, perhaps in every family it will be a parental dream for their offspring to have an M.D. or a Ph.D.

As a consequence, many parents want to postpone their kids' working years until high school, or permit it in the summer only. Or they want kids to wait until after high school, or even until after college.

That means that kids grow up used to the idea that parents

will dole out money—allowances, or cash gifts. Spending money. Which in turn takes away what an older generation grew up with—the drive and desire to get a job fast, to make some dough to pay one's own way as soon as possible.

And in the case of kids who are working, it's usually only to pay for their nearly new BMWs, car insurance, CDs, or name-brand clothes. This means that many kids today only work out of a purely materialistic desire, rather than to help support their family, as was common in the past.

So with fewer kids having an ingrained work ethic that starts manifesting itself by age ten, and with more kids than ever before getting whatever they want from their parents, hours that could be spent working are now idle hours. And idle hours frequently lead to inane hours, when silly pranks begin. When destructive deeds are done.

Success Strategies

Get Kids into Religious Activities

The easiest and best way to counteract destructive downtime is to get kids involved in religious activities: regular religious attendance, Bible study, synagogue youth group, Saturday church school, young people's choir practice, or other values-oriented gatherings. The reason religious activities are best for kids is that they provide a triple dose of what kids need desperately:

1. A good value system, which tells them how to act nobly, be unselfish, respect others, and be truthful;

2. Productive and enriching activities to occupy their time and let them mingle with like-minded kids, thus drawing them out of the loner lifestyle; and

3. Connection to a higher power, from which they can draw much strength.

That's why kids involved in weekly religious meetings, clubs, and groups receive megadoses of violence-proofing at once. They absorb good values, have their spiritual needs looked to, have fewer free hours to get into trouble, and interact with peers whose parents are also interested in their children's welfare. So, enrolling one's child in an appropriate religious facility's offerings is a must.

Interest Kids in Athletics

The next most important step to make sure kids aren't at loose ends and just waiting to get embroiled in violence is to engage them in athletics. Any sport will do, as long as the child has an interest in the activity. Parents often assume that their sports background will rub off on their kids. But that's not always the case. Just because the father played tennis in school doesn't mean the daughter will emerge as another Venus Williams.

Again, flexibility is key. All kinds of sports should be on the menu. It's best to introduce kids early to a variety of athletics, let them try several, then stick with one or two. And always leave the door open for a change of mind.

In the final analysis, few kids will become Olympic-caliber athletes, but all can find some type of physical activity they can enjoy, either in a team approach in school or after school in a private setting. And again, sports offer more than one solution to violence-proofing a child. Recent reports underline the importance of sports for girls as well as boys. For example, the May 10, 1999, issue of *10* states that girls can now "dream of

careers in pro sports . . . with plenty of female role models to follow. . . ."

Sports involvement is crucial. It builds self-esteem, cuts down
on destructive downtime, plus it lets our kids interact with other
kids on the same wavelength. Moreover, it promotes lasting positive friendships, which are desperately needed to counteract
negative ones. Athletic kids, for instance those on the volleyball
team, don't usually spend time engaged in smoking, drinking,
drugs, or sex. They're just too busy going to practice.

Encourage School Club Participation

Let's face it. Some kids aren't interested in athletic competition.
So they're the perfect candidates for other activities that exist in
our middle and high schools: school-sponsored clubs. These
range from subject-related clubs to honor-based groups to ser-
vice-oriented gatherings.

It's only a matter of finding a group or club that's a match for
your child. To begin the process, discuss the options with Kevin
and study his report card. If history is a beloved subject or music
is "really fun," all a parent has to do is investigate whether a history club or a school choir is in operation. If they are, Kevin can
check them out. If they aren't, a parent can volunteer to become
a co-sponsor. Often teachers are willing to sponsor a brand new
club if they find a parent to co-sponsor the various activities.

If that's not a possibility, many other clubs exist in today's
large schools. One simple phone call to the principal's office will
be a good start. Soon a list of special groups, from the drama
club to the office assistant's club can be perused at home and
discussed over dinner. Most kids are itching to get involved and
only need one nudge in the right direction.

In school, teachers should advertise all the various clubs and encourage their students to at least sample one meeting. A great writing assignment is this: Students, please attend one new club meeting. Then write an essay on why you will pick it or pan it.

Have Kids Join Community Clubs

If school clubs aren't an option, various community organizations for kids can be explored. Beginning with the Boy Scouts and Girls Scouts and going on to groups originating at the local YMCA or Arts Council, most communities host a plethora of gatherings for our young. To check out the possibilities, devote several afternoons to taking kids to various locations. Private swim clubs exist. Sewing classes are sponsored by fabric shops. Watercolor lessons are offered by art students supporting themselves. Piano instruction and youth orchestra opportunities are fabulous options too.

The point: Get out, scout out, and find something for Kevin, just as long as it's an activity that encourages him to be more productive and make better use of free time. Of course, summer and weekend camps by the same or similar groups should also be encouraged.

Foster Volunteer Efforts

Another great activity for kids is volunteering. That's done best by kids watching you volunteer. If you've always done pro bono work or given untold hours to the PTA or soup kitchen in your community, just take your kids along. Children love to help out. They want to give of themselves. It makes them feel terrific to be collecting teddy bears for other kids or to help Mom and Dad bake chocolate chip cookies to deliver to the homeless shelter.

If teens resist tagging along with their parents on mercy missions, they should be encouraged to seek volunteer opportunities of their own. Discuss over the dinner table what needs doing in your community. What could be more meaningful than for any family to brainstorm what a youngster can do to contribute to society?

And what's so great about the brainstorming is that kids come up with the best answers themselves. They have amazing ideas. Often they can't wait to tutor smaller kids in reading, teach senior citizens computer ABCs, share their knowledge of nature lore with kindergartners, or their skateboarding finesse with kids in an underprivileged neighborhood.

Kids can be top teachers themselves.

Of course, that may mean you're adding another volunteer job yourself because you want to supervise your kids helping other kids. In truth, parenting's pretty much full-time anyway even if you have to squeeze it in after work and on weekends. But there's nothing more heartwarming than seeing Crystal and Kevin make life better for less fortunate folks. It means your love radiates outward, like the rays of the sun.

Emphasize Hobbies

You also want to bolster your children's interests in new, exciting hobbies, so their idle hours won't become evil hours. So go ahead—pass on your knack for arts and crafts, teach them to crochet, cook gourmet dishes, or start conversing in Polish—anything to get their minds engaged, theirs hands busy, and their bottoms off the couch.

Fill Crystal and Kevin with so much joy that there's neither time nor room left for anything tragic.

The more varied interests your child has, the more he is immunized from the impulse to commit violent acts. A youngster who's collecting cards of his favorite sports team on Monday, teaching a child in a poor neighborhood about his collection of foreign stamps after school on Tuesday, reading up on arrowheads on Wednesday evening, reorganizing his bookshelves for more collectibles on Thursday, and telling his dad over pepperoni pizza on Friday about a recent new interest—dinosaurs, for example—doesn't have time to get into trouble.

Of course, on the weekend, there will be trips to card shops and stamp collection stores and exhibits or visits to the ballpark to see one's favorite team in action. Soon this busy kid will also have improved school skills, since many of his hobbies require reading, researching, and improved eye-hand coordination.

Push a Positive Internet Surfing and Media Policy

Positive Internet surfing means a youngster uses the resources of the Internet only to update herself on the latest useful Web sites or kid chat rooms. To encourage that, sit down with Crystal in front of the computer and give her a first-rate cyber-education. Teach her to examine and evaluate Web sites, games, and chat room information. Soon Crystal will know what good the Internet can do. It can be the most fabulous cyber-museum or collector's paradise. There will constantly be more to learn, to study and research, and to download. This kind of involved youngster may still be tempted to log on to trash sites and porn places from time to time. So put a screen in place. That will leave your computer-connected youngster with only one overriding goal—the quest to sniff out the latest new hot sites in her area of interest.

While you're cyber-educating your kid, help Kevin master other media messages too. Teach him to be critical of newspapers, magazines, radio and TV programs, to check ratings and contents, and to set time limits. Overall, work on developing a positive media policy for the whole family—with his help. He can scan upcoming programs, select the most acceptable shows in advance and post his very own weekly TV guide, "Kevin's Choice."

To keep Crystal and Kevin from resenting any new media rules, just "involve them in the process," advises Dr. John Murray, a child psychologist at Kansas State University.

In a short time, the ability to track down beneficial sites and access them for new information, and the empowerment kids feel when making their own TV selections in advance and broadcasting them will raise their self-esteem and standing in the eyes of classmates and friends. Other kids will stop by after school and crowd around the computer station and the TV set in your den.

Meanwhile, savvy teachers, and they all are, will capitalize on those interests and once a week toss out a computer-skill challenge that kids will spend hours to meet. And they will add a TV program-related essay question to their list of composition or journal topics for the week.

And of course, not letting a youngster have a computer or TV in his room cuts down on unsupervised Internet and mindless viewing time, which will keep your child and the others kids on a positive track.

Promote Work Experiences

One especially good way to ensure that kids develop a solid work ethic is never to give them everything they want. When they produce a birthday or holiday wish list, buy them only half, no more, and always make sure the child has a few unrealized material dreams. You want to choose the middle-of-the-road approach here, neither buy the child too much nor too little.

Leaving some "gimme-gimme" wishes unfulfilled will lead many kids to look for odd jobs so they can buy the items themselves. You certainly want to encourage their drive to stand on their own two feet. Mention small paying jobs you hear about, such as a neighbor who needs the lawn cut, an errand run, Fido walked, or a toddler looked after once in a while. Even better: Post your own chores that pay—work that has to be done around your home for which you could either hire outside help or hire your own offspring.

Soon you'll have your children asking for more paying chores (not to be confused with their regular chores, which they do as a matter of course as part of the family unit, such as cleaning their rooms, taking out trash, doing dishes, vacuuming). But for major assignments, such as conquering the attic or garage, you should pay extra. This way, you connect work and the benefit of working—getting paid—in the youngster's mind. You'll teach Crystal that working is fun and gives us a feeling of achievement. In school we work for grades; in odd jobs, for extra cash.

Both have deeper meanings, of course. In school we ultimately work to expand our mind's capacity. With chores at home, which should include some bigger ones for pay, we expand our capacity to become contributing members of society. We don't want our kids growing up as leeches. So please, encourage their interest in work; even let them have regular part-time jobs if their grades allow it. Just make sure they don't go to work in a sweatshop.

But do promote your kids' interest in working. Please. Just think about the reduction in youth violence, if all potential perpetrators had too much work to do to get warped.

Interest Kids in Internships and Shadowing

Not all part-time jobs, however, have to be paying jobs, especially for older kids. These days, other opportunities exist as well—those that are between volunteering and regular work. These include internships and shadowing. Internships allow more mature high school students, who already know what they want as future careers, to work in a professional setting one afternoon a week, not for remuneration but for training's sake.

Sometimes a youngster who shows special promise in science can find a laboratory where she can observe various procedures or do simple jobs without getting paid. She will garner valuable experience, invaluable training, and advance on her chosen path long before entering college. We are encouraged to take our daughters to work once a year. Now let's truly get our Crystals involved.

What's great about this type of internship is that is offers not only an early introduction into a complicated professional field but also allows a teen to decide for herself early on whether that it is indeed a beloved field—or not.

The same goes for shadowing, a process in which a youngster follows around an adult in a profession and observes the various facets of that field. Shadowing often works in government offices.

Parents who think their offspring might be interested in those two activities can contact the high schools where their teenagers are enrolled. Guidance departments usually provide lists of businesses interested in having a mature teen as intern or give suggestions as to how we can set up shadowing experiences ourselves.

And teachers who sense a blanket of restlessness descending on their students can talk up all kinds of work-connected opportunities.

Wouldn't it be great if parents and teachers would piece together such a quilt of true caring for all our kids, that what one side might overlook, the other side would freely supply?

Periodically Review Downtime

But whatever method we choose to make sure our children's downtime is productive, we cannot let up being vigilant, since interests and free time change frequently. As kids grow, their approach to downtime goes through many mutations. Hobbies that once satisfied, such as playing with Pokémon cards or harmless repetitive video games, don't fit the bill for an older youngster. The fact is, while kids grow taller, they expand in other directions too, in their interests. So it's extremely important to keep tabs on their free time, to overhear what they're talking to their friends about. Don't snoop, but be alert and listen to their conversations. Also observe what's going up on the walls in their rooms, what pictures are oohed and aahed over, how their notebooks are decorated. What questions they ask in class, what books and magazines they are reading.

Teachers, please, use your noodles and check their doodles.

In school libraries, parents and community leaders should

sign up for the new materials acquisition committees. What we let our kids read, we reap in the long run.

And in regards to magazines: Because of an ever stiffer competition for teen readers, some formerly conservative magazines are now leaning toward rude and crude reporting, that is, toward stories that encourage teens to become makeup mavens at twelve, wear provocative clothes at thirteen, and be sexually active at very young ages. It's as if the teen markets have become so saturated that the preteen group is now a hot commercial property.

So, please read what your kids are reading. Scan their favorite magazines even though you grew up on them. More than likely, today those magazines aren't what they used to be. Do you really want your kids to find out what their "peers" consider their most embarrassing private moments with their boyfriends? These days articles in teen 'zines abound in stories about body noises and exotic places to get pierced. How do you get your parents to cave in under pressure? What should you do with your boyfriend or girlfriend when parents are out of town? Every month, these articles are becoming more salacious.

Thus, periodically educate yourself about what your kids do in their free time, what they read, talk, and dream about, and make sure that plenty of wholesome activities are available. You can always permit your kids to get into more adult-type activities later, but you can never give them back their childhood.

Teachers have a great influence here. If they emphasize their own positive hobbies, have a show-and-tell to broadcast their own talents and artistic efforts, kids will be inspired. They can also have "trade" day. Each student demonstrates a hobby, then teaches it to a classmate, and subsequently learns a new leisure skill from his partner.

Overall, kids' talents and interests should be highlighted every day, for it's much more difficult to switch children away from destructive downtime pursuits once they're engaged in them. It's best to keep track of what they're doing to begin with and provide healthy servings of good activities for them. Offer them a mix of fun and educational time-fillers. Then they don't go looking for ways to get into trouble.

Any void in Kevin's day can be filled with either something of value and valor, or with something of vice, violence, and evil. Which do you want?

Parents and teachers, the choice is ours!

*E*vil worship. The very words send shivers down any parent's or educator's spine. How can anyone have a love for, or an allegiance to, something that's evil, bad, wicked, malevolent, or harmful? The mere combination of the word *love* with the word *evil* makes most people cringe. And to think that a child, a young human being who should be growing, learning, and striving to reach his full potential, could be involved in actual practices or thought processes revolving around such sinister behavior is even worse.

We associate hardened criminals, the worst offenders, and untreated psychiatric cases with the word *evil*. We also hear the word *evil* in church or synagogue to warn us away from sin or detrimental lifestyles. But we hardly ever associate this word with our young,

And yet, there are kids who from early on seem to have a fascination with the worst in society. They are focused on evil as if pulled by a magnet toward the underside of life. Usually those kids have been victims of tragic abuse or profound neglect themselves and have never been exposed to anything but the most horrifying experiences, to paraphrase security expert

Gavin de Becker again. In fact, his book *The Gift of Fear* cites case after case of child abuse as an indicator of kids who became killers.

That means that before those kids killed, they were corrupted.

So they're the innocent pawns of evil, rather than evil themselves. Our hearts must go out to those poor kids, and we have to help them. Before that, however, we have to learn to recognize their behaviors and all the early warning signs, so that we can move heaven and earth on their behalf.

Cruelty to Animals

One of those early warning signs is a kid's cruelty to animals. When kids kill a beloved cat just for something to do, it's a sign that something is terribly wrong. That there is violence-proneness in those kids that will erupt if we don't put a stop to it. At once. When we find that kids have no conscience, no heart, no feeling for the suffering of poor animals, we must see it as a major red flag.

Indeed, when kids capture birds, hurt them, kill them, cut them up, or play with an animal's organs, they're up to no good. That's common knowledge now. So either the kids are extremely cruel, or into demon worship, or are carrying out other evil practices.

The worst-case scenario includes signs of cruelty to animals even in a very young child. It often begins with tearing the legs off insects, goes on to shooting arrows at dogs, wounding them, and watching them die. Next may come setting bigger animals on fire, strangling them, cutting them open, sometimes while still alive. Gouging their eyes out, attacking them with objects, starving them, and watching them writhe in pain, "raping them"—the list of what cruel things a kid can inflict on animals is endless. The child doing such things is desperately crying out for help. He or she may have been victimized in the past or is being abused now.

And deliberate cruelty to animals will usually either get worse or metamorphose into cruelty to humans. So, all adults need to be on guard for any signs of cruelty to an animal, which must be dealt with immediately. Teachers also must make note of any youngster who brags about hurting an animal or who claps or cheers when watching a movie or video in which an animal is depicted in pain. Any child who laughs when a cat is run over in traffic should be checked out.

On their own, kids are kind. Only *our* negligence and cruelty make them cruel.

Demon Heroes

Another flag is the worship of demon heroes. Demon heroes are evil figures in history or current cultural icons that some kids adore. Whether those include mass murderers, torturers, or violent music makers, it is important to learn why kids adore those "bad" heroes, then do something about it. Kids are like anything else that's in the process of becoming. Whatever surrounds a work in progress colors it, right? So with kids, whatever fills their minds and hearts has a tendency to make them like it.

And the worse it is, the more power it has. Thus, when kids idolize people who are perverts, they imitate perverted behavior. Often they begin by studying the background of perverts and pick up the hobbies of those sick people. And if the kids aren't stopped, they will graduate to the same evil pursuits or the same detrimental habits of the twisted heroes they adore.

Any sign of admiration for criminals, especially violent criminals, and interest in the lives and lifestyles of prisoners, especially those who are violent, should alert us. It's one thing to have a smidgen of adoration for a clever but overall harmless crook who's managed to elude police. It's another for our kids to become occupied with vicious gangsters, mass murderers, or serial killers.

One obstacle we face with our kids' evil hero worship is that there are many borderline cases. While it's of course easy to spot kids who admire Adolf Hitler, Nazi leaders, Stalin, Lenin, or other cruel dictators from history, it's not so easy to separate the pseudo-antiheroes of today from *real* evil influences. There are now musicians, movie stars, rappers, and athletes who spout anti-values slogans only for effect. In reality they are quite nice folks and support the same family values you do. Many of those people are appalled that our kids have chosen them to be their heroes because they think these cultural icons are *against* life and normalcy. But those pseudo–bad guys wear their armor of rebelliousness only as a way to increase profits.

Thus, taken with a grain of salt, these "heroes" are harmless. It's the truly vicious people, from hate espousers to murder advocates to racists and ruthless killers, who can be a terrible influence on our children. And now we can add all the recent school killers to the list. Any youngster who expresses admiration for the nation's school shooters must be examined and redirected at once. Teachers have particularly good insight here. When they discuss school rules and routines, they must be alert to the comments of their students, especially very rebellious and destructive ones.

But instead, what often happens is that parents and teachers aren't alert. They think that any interest in historical figures or current events is something to applaud. Or they write that interest off as one of the typical weird things many kids do. Or they think it's healthy for kids to be anti-school and anti-society.

Better than my kids becoming dopeheads!

But that's not true. Both can ruin our young.

Obsession with Pseudo—Goth Culture

Goth culture is a phenomenon that has recently come to the forefront of the national scene. Unfortunately it has so many different definitions that it's hard to settle on only one. But generally it is agreed that "true Goths" are nonviolent, tolerant, frown on hatred, and enjoy their own unique style of music, literature, and art.

Yet on the fringes of their pacifistic culture, a new subculture has now spawned—the pseudo-Goths. They too seem at first harmless, like little kids dressing up for Halloween. Indeed, their absurd outfits, clothing, and other paraphernalia, and their spooky music do remind one of kids trying to scare one another, or of high schoolers or college kids getting ready for a masquerade party.

"The more outlandish, the better" seems to be their motto.

But the problem is that naive kids can quickly be sucked in by the on-the-fringe Goths. Those are people who have adopted that phenomenon with a vengeance and see it as their life's purpose not only to dress garishly, adorn themselves with chalky makeup, make sure they resemble ghosts and spooks at all times, listen to otherworldly music, and recite way off-track poetry, but also to disdain anything that could be remotely called "normal."

They even shop only in stores that feature ghoulish items, goblin masks, accessories, and incense burners.

While nothing is wrong with donning a monster outfit once a year or with putting on ghastly makeup for a trick-or-treat party, when it becomes a daily ritual to sport purple hair, black lipstick, and assorted sharp metal ornaments dangling from one's earlobes, to mimic gargoyle gazes, talk in ridiculous riddles and poems, read spooky literature, and sway to netherworldly music, our kids' growth—their inner growth especially—is retarded.

It's like trying to make healthy plants grow only in the pitch dark. Few plants can reach their potential that way. The same goes for youngsters. When their minds are cluttered with images of witches and warlocks and their attention is constantly focused on dungeon and dragon games or other fake Goth goals, their normal growth pattern is hampered. No child can grow up healthy and productive as long as her attention is riveted only on ghoulish things.

Little kids wake up screaming from nightmares. Often after they've seen a frightening movie they have terrible dreams. That's all right as long as it occurs only once in a while. But why should anyone deliberately overload a child's imagination with gruesome images and frightening music? And with visions of horror?

So, kids' far-out fashions, fetishes, fads, music, literature, and other aspects of life that copy the pretend-Goth culture must be made note of, then phased out of their lives. The sooner the better. Let's delete those negatives.

Violent Hobbies

The same goes for violent hobbies. Violent hobbies often start out as harmless leisure activities, but unless stopped, they can escalate to serious problems. This begins with constant verbal fighting and progresses to physical assault. Kids turn on each other, view one another as enemies, and live only to punch, attack, bite, or bully a smaller youngster.

Often that can happen in families in which a parent or step-parent is violent or where kids are being abused by a relative or neighbor. Or when parents refuse to acknowledge the problem and stop it.

Other times, unfortunately, parents' forms of discipline include beatings and/or verbal abuse. Of course, kids who are spanked, berated, and belittled a lot, are called "idiots" and deliberately embarrassed, will develop a "mean" gene. In fact, coming from a violent background encourages violent behavior in children.

Thus, our children's surroundings and hobbies are important and must be observed. Even if kids only threaten one another but do it often, we must be alert. Constant threats denote a serious problem, as do "fun" fistfights that kids engage in and claim do not hurt their partners. Additionally, frequently imitating pro wrestling and other violent sports should raise red flags.

The key is noticing how much time is spent wrestling or fighting. If it happens more than occasionally, take notice. Also playing "war" with pretend battles or violent video games with fancy techno-gadgets, or watching gory movies more than once in a while, must wake us up. What kids do frequently fashions them.

We should also pay attention to the music and reading

materials our kids prefer: Hate music and hate poetry are items to worry about if they seem to be a habitual pastime. Teachers should check their reading lists and delete any literature that espouses violence, especially in the early grades.

Success Strategies

Pay Attention

With this warning sign, again our kids themselves are our best helpers. They give us every reason and opportunity to check on their degree of attraction to violence. All we have to do is watch.

Like animals leave tracks, so our kids, on their way to dangerous pursuits, leave plenty of signs all over—in vicious letter writing, hate sign markings, verbal and physical threats over the phone and in e-mail, intimidation of others, setting up of dangerous experiments (which they will always claim are for school), constant speeding once they get their licenses, and racing motorcycles at night without lights.

Kids truly are open books. We just need to read them with concentration, with comprehension. We need to look at them carefully as we would study a rare book's illustrations. So, please, parents and teachers, give the kids in your care the once-over frequently.

Really, *really* look at them. Look at their dear little faces, their arms. Do they have bruises and bite marks? Wounds that don't heal? Watch out for those. Indeed, any signs of physical harm or any continued fighting among kids or the frequent use of extreme swear words, racial slurs, and threats has to be noticed.

Harm won't come to our kids if we halt it. Even kids who have become embroiled in evil activities and have switched from being thrilled over good deeds, which is their natural state, to being thrilled over pain, an unnatural state, can be helped.

It begins with finding the cause.

Identify the Cause

Why does the child adore bad people or act out bad behaviors? If violence and abuse at home are ruled out, older siblings who may not live at home, friends, relatives, neighbors, school personnel, coaches, scout leaders, and church or other staff must be examined.

Who has harmed this darling child? must be the question, and we can't rest until the answer is found.

The reason: A child who hasn't been hurt deeply or who doesn't frequently watch hurt being inflicted on others or is made to participate in demon rites, witch practices, or similar toxic behaviors does not on his own turn into a bad seed.

Kids are born pure and good.

But kids who have been forced to participate in badness often can't help themselves. They act out those bad behaviors. They're like trees that have been twisted as saplings by a tornado and grow up warped. So we must make every effort to keep all kids away from adult predators. From the moment they can talk, kids everywhere must be taught to report whatever and whoever hurts them. Otherwise, they might eventually act out what has happened to them. And they must be taught that it's not only their peers who can harm them but older people too. Not all adults can be trusted, no matter how friendly they act.

Also, a complete examination of the child in question is always in order whenever we find one whose interests have become twisted. This must include a medical checkup and a psychological evaluation. Next the root causes of the child's abnormal conduct must be removed quickly. Only after the child has been rescued from the abusive or perverted lifestyle can he be helped. To see to that, we must start over from scratch—that is, go back to how kids learn to admire good heroes and make sure we supply plenty of those.

Introduce Real Heroes

The reason kids get so enamored with vicious gangsters and serial killers is because we adults let them, either by omission or by setting a bad example ourselves. So first we must do our best to be good people, live good lives, admire goodness wherever we find it, and praise it openly. Then we must make sure our kids get to know some real heroes. Of course, we can't check up on all of today's sports heroes and movie stars to see if they're as good as they sound in the media, but we can talk about the qualities that make people real heroes.

We can also direct our offspring toward people we considered our heroes when we were young. We can encourage kids to read about and study the lives of historical figures whose actions and contributions have withstood the test of time. Who can deny the courageous and noble qualities of an Abe Lincoln, a Florence Nightingale, a Jesse Owens, or a Sacajawea? Let's tell our kids about Sophie and Hans Scholl, two students who dared to take on Hitler!

In this area, we have such a wide choice of options. We can include true heroes of all ethnic backgrounds, make sure males and females are equally represented, help our kids interview other adults as to their opinions of heroic qualities, and have lively discussions on truly heroic lives.

Moreover, there are numerous books, from fascinating biographies to novels, that deal with recognized heroes. Reference works in which genuine heroes are heralded abound in print and electronic form. What we want to do is make our offspring focus on people, past and present, whose qualities are truly admirable. We want to immerse Kevin and Crystal in the stories of those who have saved whole countries, fought major battles, gave their lives in the fight against evil.

And what a splendid opportunity this is for child care workers, teachers, and religious leaders to educate our youngsters about the finest people who ever lived! All those great heroes and saints of the past and present! When we introduce our kids to them, we light bright, inextinguishable candles.

Change Kids' Direction

In order for kids to lose interest in outlandish behaviors, way-out activities, music, and violent games, they need to be redirected to fun pursuits. And when you do that, you can almost feel their relief. Wow! Once they realize that there is a world of normalcy just waiting for them and in which they are now included, you can sense their immense joy.

It's difficult for most kids to have to sneak around their parents and teachers to join a demon-worshiping cult which requires that they dress outlandishly or in black outfits every day. But once that heavy burden is lifted, kids are like new. They really want to be rescued. That's why they show their pull toward sinister "heroes" so openly in the first place—to get the attention of one caring adult. Just one! Then what a good feeling it is for them to be just kids again, not pseudo-warriors trying to cause mischief, fighting all the time, or having to cause pain. It's hard for kids to swim against the river of goodness by always having to be "bad."

But now they're in the light again and can heal and grow, which opens the door to so many healthy pursuits.

The trick is to find some terrific activities to replace their violent hobbies. That takes time and energy, but there are many options. Just look at whatever occupied them before you intervened in the violence-prone youngster's life. If Crystal thrived on Goth-style music, help her find music that isn't violent but is still cutting edge or "hot" or "cool," or whatever the current adjective may be.

If Kevin has posters of neo-Nazis plastered on his wall, tear them down, then help him choose appropriate posters and reading materials. Or if your teen has spent time logging on violent Internet sites, connect him with peers who despise such sites. Any normal group of youngsters will do, as long as your child can find something in common with them.

Even the most evil-entrenched kid has a smidgen of admiration for mega–sports heroes like Michael Jordan or Mia Hamm. So begin with that smidgen of good hero worship. Build on it by providing pictures, books, and articles on that superb athlete. Then grow it by talking about or by stressing the winning qualities in that idol.

Of course, it's always best to involve the child in the selection of new heroes and new activities. Fortunately there are so many records, CDs, comic books, posters, video games, movies, and good video games on the market now that the choices are unlimited. And in the process of helping your kid choose new and better allegiances, you'll discover Crystal's and Kevin's true talents, which do not include a talent for evil.

Recognize Their Talents

To extract a child from violence means to get to know his strengths and help him connect to them. Don't dwell on past mistakes, but rather start over. That means you pretend this child is new to your family and you want to offer him every advantage, every opportunity. So observe what he seems to enjoy and what he dislikes, then strengthen the likes toward positive pursuits, and avoid the dislikes.

Should Crystal express just a hint of interest in ice hockey, take her to a game, buy her a Carolina Hurricanes sweatshirt, finagle an introduction to a professional ice hockey player, let her traipse on the ice herself one Saturday morning and watch some of her peers totter around and chase after a puck while others glide like swans across the mirror-like surface. Then take her to a sports emporium and have her check on the price of skates, encourage her to research the history of hockey on the Internet or the Olympic stars in that field—whatever seems to pique her. Get Crystal to "think, dream, eat, and sleep" ice hockey from now on. Or horseback riding. Or tap dancing.

Or maybe Kevin would rather dive into martial arts. Whatever gets him excited has to be fine with you as long as it's not demonic.

Enlist the help of your kid's teachers. Kids thrive when their parents and teachers are on the same team. Teachers can have interesting books "on reserve" in the school library waiting for Kevin to peruse them. They can be on high alert during all the hours when parents aren't around. Thus, Kevin's recovery back to the happy, good boy he used to be—the happy, good boy that's still in him, only shrouded over now—can be shared.

Stay Alert

Unlike a broken foot, however, you can't expect a child's soul that's been damaged to heal in three or six weeks or six months. It will probably take as long or longer as the abuse went on or as long as she has been practicing cruel acts.

So don't expect to change a child who's been seriously mistreated overnight. Years of difficult work may be needed. There may be occasions of backsliding or weeks when it seems hopeless. You may think you have your teenager cured from her adulation for a serial killer or an international assassin only to find her fascinated by sadism or masochism. But don't ever give up. On the contrary, just as you would keep administering medicine to a child who's diabetic or suffers from asthma, so will you have to hang in there with a child who shows serious signs of abuse, which she may act out by abusing others.

Team Up with Pros

It's incredible how much help is at our fingertips. All we have to do is ask for it. In the case of a youngster who has been demonized by his surroundings and turned away from goodness, outside help is especially readily available and needed. Ask the school to back you up in your efforts. Teachers want to help—that's their nature.

However, so many parents take their kids for a visit or two to a school counselor or psychologist, then expect an instant cure. Again, that's not going to happen. Kids whose injuries run deep need time and the best treatment available.

So after having Kevin and Crystal tested and after removing the cause of their abnormal behaviors, make sure you keep taking them for their appointments with the appropriate professionals. Same goes for the parents. For having a child who has a heart defect is a terrible blow.

When kids are engulfed in the love of evil, they are youngsters with the worst possible heart defects. Not physical ones, of course, but spiritual ones. Naturally that's a tremendous shock to any family. Yet feeling shame at not having been vigilant enough earlier doesn't solve the problem. Parents and teachers should never blame themselves for not having seen the early signs of evil in a kid.

Just as kids are not to blame for having been ensnared in a web of badness, so adults are not to blame for what they did not see. But once they do, they must spring into action. They must make sure that kids are counseled and helped from then on. That's best done in concert with experts who will have specific recommendations beyond the basic ones mentioned here.

Praise for Achievement

Just as adults want recognition and praise, so do kids, especially those with injured souls. And as you now re-raise that hurt child who has already experienced far more bad things than she should have, remember what I said earlier:

A cruel or abusive child usually has been in some cruel or abusive surrounding. You must offset that by offering plenty of praise for every small achievement. For every good day or week that passes, plan something special that shows your youngster that you're proud of the recovery from violence or destructive behavior that she's making. For every good and normal step she takes, shower her with appreciation. Make a list of positive comments and use them each day, no matter how hard you have to try. Don't fall into a repetitive mode of saying "Good job" over and over. Network with other parents and friends to come up with novel laudatory expressions, then use them freely. Crystal may tense when you praise her in a particular way because she may associate your genuine compliment with something her former abuser said when he took advantage of her. So delete that statement from your list, but keep saying nice things to her anyway, without expecting anything from her in return.

Can you picture an injured puppy? First it may growl when you bring it a delicious dog crunchy. But after a while it may accept food without growling. Some time later it may actually wag its tail and permit you to rub its fluffy fur, its soft little belly. Same with deeply hurt kids. First they won't trust any adult, no matter who. But slowly, over time, they will let a parent or teacher come closer.

For it's in the nature of kids to heal, and all kids are resilient. A damaged little soul can be difficult to make all better, though take comfort in this: At least the problem has been caught before it was too late, and you were instrumental in that.

Expect Success

Focus on what *can* be done. Also keep in mind that an abused child, a deliberately cruel child, or a constantly aggressive child hasn't had a childhood or not much of one. So tell him right away that things will get better. Be absolutely positive in this: Things will get better for sure.

Being a victim of abuse as a child doesn't mean one has to remain a victim. And being a bully doesn't mean you have to keep being one. And being filled with hate doesn't mean you have to keep hating. And loving evil doesn't mean you can't change.

For you can. Our children can. Our world can. There are many ways to overcome evil.

Kids grow every day, and as they do, they grow inside. They become better. And nature has a way of healing all hurts. Indeed, scars can fade fast on the outside, and be "loved off" on the inside by truly committed parents, teachers, and other adults. It takes a solid commitment to "refit or retrofit" a child, but it's possible. Many, many kids go through a fascination-with-evil stage without any lasting harm. Most don't become hardened criminals. They grow up into fine human beings, so please take heart.

Remember also: Many kids in the past were beaten mercilessly. That didn't turn them all into wife beaters or child abusers. Or school shooters.

Otherwise all the kids who saw nothing but war in their early years would be real war-mongers. And all those World War II survivors, myself included, would crave violence. They would be out for each other's blood constantly, but that's not the case.

Even the most violence-entrenched kid is salvageable. All it takes is a parent or teacher to make the effort to notice the signs of violence-proneness and to fight against them.

That takes us to the last and most serious sign.

Sign 8: Future Limbo

*L*imbo refers to a state of confusion or neglect, and *future limbo* is a state in which an individual lacks future plans to such an extent that he feels the world is coming to an end. That's a terrible condition for anyone, because it tends to paralyze the individual. If you can't even see a hint of a path ahead, you're tempted to stop moving. Most likely you freeze.

This happened to me in 1961 when I first came to America and found myself terribly sick and stranded in New York City. I was so weak I had to sit down on the curb. Cars whizzed past me, dusting me. I didn't know a soul, had all of 95 cents in my pocket, and had no idea what to do next. For thirty minutes I was suspended in a terrifying limbo, but finally I dragged myself up and eventually made it to Grand Central Station. To catch a train south. . . .

My limbo state was only temporary, and I was twenty-one years old. But nowadays future limbo is a permanent state for many of our young kids. They experience a dreadful feeling each and every day, but theirs never lets up, and they don't know what to do. Where to turn. How to make it another day.

What makes this especially serious is that kids depend on their futures. That's all they have really—the hours, days, weeks, months, and years to come—all those terrific times yet to be, for their pasts are too short to matter. Future limbo is a terrible state for a child to endure.

There can be many reasons that kids find themselves trapped in this awful state, but the most prevalent reason is their toxic relationship to school. That can easily be avoided, especially since future limbo doesn't come out of nowhere. Usually it creeps in slowly over a child's school years.

To be helpful, parents and other concerned caregivers need to recognize the true cause of future limbo, validate its existence, then deal with it. Once and for all.

The Closed-Door Syndrome

If the symptoms of school alienation mentioned in chapter 7 aren't recognized and treated in a child's early school years, a shutting down of options occurs in high school. This is known as the "closed-door syndrome."

It means that year after year, certain academic pathways are shut off from some youngsters as they fail to keep up. For example, if they don't have knowledge of, or competency in, a foreign language or certain science or prerequisite math, they can't advance along with their peers. Middle and junior high and high schools present coursework that builds upon the previous year's study. Thus, if a student and his parents are not alert, many college options will not be available. Then the academic doors slam shut in a teenager's face, and his world begins to collapse. Feelings of worthlessness (not because of a lack of "smarts" but because of not having paid attention to detail or having over-looked various requirements at the proper time) set in.

There is no worse feeling for any kid than to have no future, especially if he comes from a family that has great plans for their offspring. High-achieving families always make matters worse, in this case. Also, if the student is enrolled in a demanding series of courses, yet has failed to learn even the minimum required, that has to be an awful experience for any student. He suddenly realizes he doesn't have the skills and knowledge to take the same path as the rest of the class. He's simply out.

Often the PSAT in sophomore year is a wake-up call for students of this type. But one test can be laughed off, especially when the student is still hanging on by passing grades. Crystal can always explain away a low PSAT or another important pre-college exam score by saying she didn't try or care.

Her next wake-up call is the SAT or other more advanced achievement tests that juniors and seniors take. When these result in very low scores too, at the same time Crystal's grades are of a barely passing caliber, she may react like a deer caught in the headlights of a truck. In genuine despair, she will not know what to do next.

Should she start studying now, or is it too late? Should she run away? But where to, in heaven's name? Or should she just stay in school and be miserable? Meanwhile classmates brag about their top scores. Signs sprout on bulletin boards in high schools all over the country declaring where others have been accepted—at the local university, or the fine out-of-state college, or that Ivy League school or small expensive place in Virginia their parents graduated from.

Soon all the student's friends are talking college while Kevin has nowhere to go. That's when limbo feelings magnify, and often a death wish begins to materialize. Feelings of shame, intermingled with frustration and a loss of hope, combine to make a teenager either want to lash out violently against others or do away with himself in a violent way.

Poor Kevin!

The worst combination is the even more frequent desire to do both at once—to strike out against those more successful while at the same time ending one's own miserable existence. In the long run, the feeling of limbo that comes with being boxed in at school is so unbearable that the teen focuses only on what he believes is a logical final conclusion.

Suicidal Thoughts

The reason kids in desperate straits think of suicide first is that their short lifespans have ill equipped them to come up with other solutions. "Adolescents don't think like adults and react with gut instinct when they process emotions," says Deborah Yurgelun-Todd, M.D., director of neuropsychology and cognitive neuro-imaging at the Harvard Medical School McLean Hospital Brain Imaging Center. They seem hot-tempered and spacy, when in reality "their brains aren't yet developed enough to encode what we're saying and hold on to it." So kids tend to tune adults out and do rash things. In despair, they choose the last resort as their first option.

And this problem is growing. To quote the American Academy of Child and Adolescent Psychiatry, teen suicides have increased drastically in the last few years: "Suicide is the third leading cause of death for 15- to 24-year-olds, and the sixth leading cause of death for 5- to 14-year-olds."

It's also easier for a youngster than for an adult to kill herself because emotions can run wild in children. Their feelings of shame can be overwhelming. The worst thing that can happen to kids is to be ridiculed by their group of close friends. And that can happen to bright youngsters who have messed up royally in their academics.

For a teenager, suicide can take on a romantic or idealized hue. It's seen as a heroic deed or an act of revenge on classmates, parents, teachers, coaches, the church or synagogue. The student thinks that her friends, family, and others will be sorry when they find her dead, and spends much time fantasizing about that vision. She composes good-bye letters mentally or actually types them on the computer, and gloats over visions of parents and teachers dissolved in tears.

Also, today's movies, music, video games, and other media can lead many a youngster to believe that suicide is a glorious experience. Therefore, Crystal's idea of suicide is based on unrealistic views. Plus, with access to weapons, pills galore in her parents' medicine cabinet, or with drugs easily available, an overdose seems no more difficult than popping a couple aspirins and going to sleep on the couch. And firing a gun seems like cartoon action, not reality.

Poor Crystal!

Additionally, some kids truly believe that their parents would be better off if they weren't around. Maybe they've overheard arguments concerning themselves, or they have recently recognized that they're different from the rest of the family. They feel that they will never measure up. That they are just bad. All those things combine to point toward suicide as the only way out. For that reason, this is a very perilous time in a youngster's life, because suicidal thoughts usually don't stop by themselves.

Instead, unless intervention takes place, they escalate until the youngster has a profound death wish.

Death Wish

A death wish is just like any other wish for kids—something they desire or long for. It's a definite goal, like getting that first car. Except in this case it's death they desire.

And from the death wish it's only a short step to the carrying out of that wish. Since kids want everything right now, they do not carry around with them a yen to die for years. No. They do something about it right away. Postponing gratification is never one of children's strengths, particularly not of those who find themselves in these straits. They act out what's on their minds without the filter of maturity or the damper of thought.

And not only will they scheme and prepare to do away with themselves, they will also often plot how to "wipe out" others, for instance, classmates who may have slighted them, a teacher who may have given them a D, or parents who have denied them the use of the family car or made them stick to a curfew.

Or didn't pay attention to them!

In the confused state kids find themselves when all they see is closed doors, they're like cornered rats that attack anyone coming near. Thus, they blow out of proportion the smallest disregards or hurts while moving inexorably toward their one goal—erasing their existence.

In truth, they're dear but desperate kids whose thinking has become so twisted that they can't see straight any more. In their deep-feeling souls, they wish someone would rescue them. They frantically want to undo their past mistakes, all the times they didn't study their irregular verbs, hand in those term papers, take notes in biology class, and listen to their instructors.

Oh, how they wish someone would help them now! But they are too proud, too ashamed, too embarrassed, too tongue-tied, too confused, too warped, or too incapable in their thinking to confide in anyone and ask for help. So they suffer daily in silence while inexorably preparing for the end—their own and maybe that of a few of their peers as well. Or of many. They may even use a calculator to tally up the hundreds of classmates they hope to blow up.

But what they really want is to live and become the fine persons that reside deep within them. But now, pressed desperately against the wall, they don't want not to have mattered at all. According to Teen Help Adolescent Resources (see the Resource Guide, page 185), in the next twenty-four hours, 1,439 teens will attempt suicide. Some will resort to speeding and crashing their automobiles or motorcycles or to taking huge overdoses of drugs. Or truly wanting to go out like a comet shooting across the sky, they may open fire on completely innocent kids in their school cafeteria or lobby and target crowds that have excluded them or that they think excluded them.

Just so they will be remembered. Forever. If not for their good deeds, then for their evil ones.

Success Strategies

Remediate Weaknesses

Remediation is overcoming learning disabilities or problems with scholastics. Early on in the child's schooling, steps must be taken to ensure a child's successful progress. In middle school also, a youngster's advancement in academics must be monitored. But especially in high school, close attention must be paid to a teen's achievement. That's easily done by checking report cards.

But so often parents of teenagers feel that schoolwork supervision is unnecessary. Kids at that age chafe against adults who hover. So why bother?

Yet it's precisely at this time that students can fall through the cracks, often because they haven't mastered necessary skills and concepts. When, for instance, an elementary knowledge of the parts of speech (nouns, verbs, adjectives, adverbs) isn't mastered by the middle grades, a student will not be able to make much progress in a foreign language, since all foreign language training beyond mere conversation requires a background in grammar.

The same is true for advanced math and science courses. If basic concepts were never truly incorporated by the end of sixth or seventh grade, the sophomore and junior will have trouble not only in trigonometry or calculus, but also in physics and chemistry.

So parents must patiently pinpoint the root causes for low grades and see to it that their kids get all learning gaps filled. And teachers must patiently reteach the basics their students are missing.

Hire Private Teachers

Sometimes, however, a regular teacher has a strike against her when she tries to get a student caught up. The reason is that it's frustrating to teach one's heart out every day, only to have several or many students fail the culminating exam. So there's a feeling of frustration on the teacher's part and a feeling of embarrassment on the failing student's part. Neither is conducive to patient explanations and smooth relearning.

But a private teacher can cut right through the tense atmosphere. He has no past connection with the student, and only positive goals ahead—to get the pupil to advance. So the student is given a new chance to impress the instructor, while the instructor can concentrate on only one charge—and get him up to par scholastically. Kevin gets another chance to catch up. And he will!

Examine Goals

Many parents may begin their parenting with an easy-to-rear first child—a quiet, studious, adult-oriented little person who looks so darling and likes to listen and learn. That's all the training parents get—the easy parenting mode when all goes well. But subsequent children don't follow the same path. They can be more sociable, more active, and less adult-oriented, since they see the world peopled by their peers. After all, their older sibling is there to interact with. Thus, the more kids parents have, the more varied their brood may be in learning styles and personalities.

For that reason, parents can't ever use a cookie-cutter approach and treat their kids as if they all came from the same mold. But unfortunately, many parents aren't flexible enough to realize that just because they have three girls or three boys, all three don't have the same scholastic talents.

Yet parents must wake up and get to know their kids as individuals, appreciate them for who they are, not for who the parents wish they were, and raise them in the kids' best interests, not their own. To do that requires periodically examining goals with your youngsters and asking questions about what they wish to do some day, then guiding them toward attainable goals. It's never a good idea to just "assume" one's offspring will attend one's alma mater or the tough university Older Sister attended. For too much pressure results in only one thing—in the case of an old-fashioned, overheated pressure cooker, a blown lid and beef stew spattered on the ceiling. Or in the case of a tortured teen, it may result in his resorting to the worst solution possible.

Notice Danger Signs of Suicide

For kids, the worst solution is often shrouded in romantic colors. They aren't frozen by fear before they take that last step, even though we wish and pray fear would freeze them. But most suicidal kids just march toward their goal, step by step. On and on. It's a lark, once they've decided in their own mind or in discussion with close friends that suicide is the best option.

Fortunately, there are many warning signs. Some of them are sudden changes in a teen's behavior. For example, if a formerly messy kid becomes super-neat overnight. Or if a kid given to temper outbursts becomes exceptionally calm and easy to get along with, starts doling out his favorite CD collection, bestows his beloved mountain bike on a kid brother, and acts withdrawn or disengaged from interests that formerly were very dear to his heart, a parent should investigate what's going on.

Other warning signs include talking about killing oneself, leaving notes about it, changing eating and other habits drastically, becoming melancholy, withdrawing from family, constantly being bored, adopting a different personality, spending hours listening to music by groups that advocate suicide, continuously reading poetry by young writers who have killed themselves, or in general rhapsodizing about the beauty of death.

Hey, wouldn't the world be so much better off without me?

Parents must know those signs and whatever new ones crop up, so that they can spot them easily. It's therefore most important for parents to keep their eyes on their kids. Frequently, however, parents think they must only watch toddlers for every move, so they won't stick their fingers in a socket, swallow dimes, or poke peas up their noses. Then as the kids get older, they relax. Too much.

What they must do instead is become more acute observers of *all* their kids, no matter what age. Anyone can make sure a two-year-old doesn't dart into the street. Just lock the gate or hold tight on to the child's hand. That's easy. But parents of older kids must develop keen insight. Parenting is not an entry-level job with skills that don't need upgrading. Parents must grow with their kids and become ever more alert.

And all teachers should know the suicide warning signs. A kid bent on killing herself is apt to do that, plus take others along. Increased alertness may bring us to intervene.

Along with increasing their alertness, parents and teachers must make observations about what they see, write them down, then act on them. In truth, so many parents and teachers who have kids in that confused, pushed-against-the-wall state know something's wrong. They have an "uneasy" feeling, yet are afraid to face it. They are too embarrassed to report their deepest worries to someone who could help—the school's guidance counselor, or a doctor, psychologist, or child psychiatrist.

Teachers can be cowards too. Some, but by no means all, fear being singled out as having suicidal students. They think it's a blemish on their spotless careers to have despondent kids in class. So they shut their eyes and close their hearts until it's too late.

Parents also push their feelings of unease aside, remembering their own early years when they were confused. Or maybe they are just so busy with their own lives that they don't take time to follow up on their hunches and deal with them.

Today's family configurations include single parents raising kids and melded families raising stepkids. In all those cases, day-to-day living is complicated by the many new and ever-present complexities. Therefore, few parents really have the time required to examine the behavior of their offspring. In the rush of getting their own work done and the household seen to, they're up to their necks already in a sea of difficulties. So as long as their teens don't vandalize their neighbors' house, get arrested, or pester them too much, Mom and Dad are pretty content.

But that's exactly when troubled kids fall by the wayside. They feel they would only complicate their parents' lives if they'd open up to them, not that they would know how to start. Or they think their own parents are in even worse trouble themselves, they way they have to dose themselves every day with Prozac, stiff drinks, cigarettes, and who knows what else. So why bug them?

But all parents must shelve their own miseries for later and have clear eyes for their offspring. And all teachers, please be on the alert. Only then can you recognize the desperate signs of kids with a death wish.

Get Professional Advice

If you spot those signs, or if you have any inkling that all isn't well with Crystal, it's best to get professional help at once. Forget what the neighbors will say, what relatives and friends will think. When a child exhibits even just one suicide danger sign, help must arrive fast. You wouldn't let your kids drag around with a "busted" knee. You rush them to the emergency room. Neither would we allow a child with a cough, fever, and sore throat to blithely skip along. No, we make sure a doctor checks her and prescribes medicine.

In the same way, a youngster who shows a fascination with death or acts in a death-defying way by frequent speeding, getting drunk, taking drugs, pills, or inhalants, or by doing any of the many things that present a *real* danger to their lives, is also in need of help. In all those cases, help must come quickly.

Parents often think that if they don't produce "normal" teenagers, they're failures. Rather than face the fact that maybe they didn't do a 100 percent perfect job in raising a child, they try to keep the troublesome youngster under wraps. They prefer to sweep all problems with their kids under the rug, hoping that they will go away. But teenagers who have no future mapped out don't ever consider "outgrowing" their problems a solution. They want to resolve the difficulty. Now. And parents must remember that.

In truth, maybe some children do overcome their suicidal inclination when they become adults. *If* they become adults, that is. But who wants to take the chance that they may not reach adulthood?

Some teachers also try to whitewash kids' behaviors. Who wants to hassle Kevin over his most recent journal entry about wanting desperately to be in a better place soon? It's scary territory to talk to him about more than the A– he got, that comma splice, those dangling participles. . . .

But often the real reason teachers don't get involved with borderline suicidal cases in their classes is that sometimes their principals have boxed them in. "How is counseling Kevin going to make the state test scores go up?" they demand. "It's student achievement that matters!"

Not student agonies!

Yet we all must break that vicious cycle in which our kids believe the only way out is death—theirs, and maybe a few others'.

Encourage Therapy—Group and Individual

Fortunately many high schools recognize that kids can become cornered to such an extent that they consider suicide. These schools offer programs to help, from individual counseling to group sessions. The problem with these is that high schools are small towns. Few kids want to be seen visiting the guidance counselor or school psychologist. Older kids can be cruel. They call each other "crazy" even without the stigma of having been in the guidance department for anything other than picking up a college application.

Furthermore, kids don't have time during their school day to visit the counselor's office. Every hour there means missing the calculus class they so desperately need, since most of the time scholastic failure is the major cause for their deep despair.

Private therapy is a wiser approach. It can be scheduled after school or on Saturday mornings. In a group setting there, it isn't as likely that one's classmates will be in the same group and will blab. Or make faces if the teen tries to unburden herself.

That doesn't solve the problem of getting the youngster to agree to see a professional. On the contrary, most kids in trouble probably won't agree to visit a psychiatrist. So the parent should first go alone, report his observations, and garner tips and suggestions to use at home to help "lift" the kid out of the depths of her gloom.

Sometimes a reward may propel a teenager to accompany a parent to a counseling sessions. Then, once the ice is broken, the teenager may go alone. However, it's never a simple process to get help for a teen who's been left to flounder for years until she thinks all exits are barred and the only way out is by tragic means.

Yet, even in the worst scenario, a parent who concentrates on getting help for a troubled child, who tries different methods and different professionals, who asks for referrals and puts his own life on hold for a few months or even a few years, can win the battle.

Affirm Life

What helps more than anything is to have a positive outlook on life.

Kids pick up many obvious characteristics from their parents, but even more important, they're aware of the smallest hues and trends. So when a parent is pessimistic or makes comments about how hard life is, how unfair and how sad most people's existence is, she sows negative seeds that can come to fruition in her kid's suicide.

Parents should always be positive, find solutions, and instill in their children the belief that failure is only an opportunity to try again. And parents should be very careful when discussing suicide and never hold it up as a quick fix. If they praise a person who killed himself, they make a hero out of a coward, for killing oneself is always a cowardly way out. Living, especially under tough circumstances, takes guts. But taking one's life is a wimpy "solution," that is, a selfish reaction that should *enrage* us, not make us applaud.

And teachers should never glorify the suicide of a poet, a writer, a figure in history. Kids so believe their teachers that they might think their own suicide will earn them the respect they crave.

What we need to do as adults is to tell our kids that it's wrong to even consider suicide. Life is a gift that demands a lot from us, but the fact we're alive means we have within us the capabilities to surmount any obstacle that comes along.

In our classrooms and in the rehashing of news at home, we must always discuss what the men or women who killed themselves could have done to triumph over their problems. We must not only provide food, clothing, a roof, and education for our kids; we must cultivate a life-affirming outlook for ourselves, then transmit it to our kids. That's most important. We grown-ups may not all have the "happiness gene," but we all have the capacity to act like we're happy or at least act confidently and trust in the future. If need be, we must work at being optimistic, so we can pass on that positive attitude. Teachers should always teach hopefulness along with history and heritage lessons.

In the final analysis, what helps our children more than the mountains of material things we shower them with is our ability to bounce back. If we give that to our youngsters, we make them immune from utter hopelessness. As long as they have trust in the future, they're not going to end their lives or those of their peers, teachers, or parents.

Indeed, there's no greater gift than the gift of hope. We must feed our children heaping spoonfuls of it every day.

Care and Connect Daily

Kids know deep in their hearts when we truly care about them. They know that, even more than by what we provide for them, by how much time we spend with them and by what we do during our time together. Although no child wants to be poor, thousands of poor kids grow up feeling loved. At the same time thousands of rich kids grow up feeling undesired. They have tons of toys, gobs of gadgets, and caches of cash and clothes, but they're desperately unhappy.

Money does not equal love. Never has, never will.

The key to caring is how much of ourselves we are willing to give, how much of our hearts we're willing to share. We give very little when we rush past Kevin and Crystal in the morning, snap a question at them in the evening, then fly out the door again to a meeting only to see them very briefly again the next morning and hardly any time on weekends. We have to prioritize differently from now on, because kids aren't just appliances we switch on and off, or paintings we display on our walls, or expensive leather furniture we showcase in our greatrooms.

No, kids are like us, with their own personalities, potentials, and problems. So we must shove aside our own quest for success, our stampede for the best stock options, and our career concerns, at least as much as possible.

We must sit down and talk to our kids every day, a minimum of fifteen minutes to half an hour per child, and much longer on the weekends.

And if that's not possible? Make it possible.

Today's modern lifestyles have made it so much easier to connect with our kids on a daily basis. We can now do laundry in half an hour, cook up plenty in fifteen minutes, and clean up in no time if everyone pitches in. Or, if the budget permits, have someone come in and do it for us. We can network with other parents to run errands, carpool, and have a common homework hour that's supervised by a dad down the street one day a week. The next day it's your turn.

With both parents working, frequently more income is available. So what stops us from having supper catered? Or picking up salads and subs on the way home? Or having the baked chicken prepared by the stay-at-home mom down the street one week, while you concoct double portions of broccoli with cheese sauce, for you and them, the following week?

Fortunately, with modern technology, connecting with your child every day is easier than ever. You can use cell phones and pagers to stay in touch, and most important, e-mail your child every day from work. Next to your own voice, a written message shows how much you care and how important that young life is to you.

The fact that you're a parent at the start of the new millennium means you're fully able to manage your life in such a manner that you can be a terrific mom or dad. Just remember, it's the kids that count. Everything else can be seen to later.

You can always develop a dream career once the kids are grown. You can pick up college degrees later. You can update your wardrobe in years to come, and decorate your abode in five, ten, fifteen years. You can go on a diet, exercise like a maniac well into your middle years. Get back to that size 6 if that's your heart's desire.

But there's one thing you can never do over, no matter how much you try, how many people you command, how many millions you throw around. That one thing, once it's gone, is gone forever—and that is raising your dear children into productive and caring adults.

So postpone what you have to. Be ruthless about it. Your life has many decades, but you only have about twenty years to rear that most precious gift you'll ever have—your own daughter, your own son.

Save your children. You'll be saving the best part of yourself. Your kids are your link to immortality.

All kids want desperately to be rescued from their spiral of violence. They silently beg and plead with their parents and teachers and all adults they meet to save them from the downward slope.

We do that by not overlooking their problems. From the moment a child enters child care and later school, there is a unique opportunity for each educator who interacts with this child to make him better. According to Kenneth Dodge, director of Duke University's new Center for Child and Family Policy, "By the time they [kids] are 4 years old, they already display aggressive behavior problems. We can do things to prevent these [violent] outbursts." He couldn't be more correct.

From the beginnings of the American educational system, schools have always had more than the mere emphasis on academics as their duty. They've also had character training and the imparting of noble ideals in their lesson plans, as well as the safety of our young. So, schools must continuously keep step with emerging trends. What good is it to bemoan the fact that our kids are getting worse, then throw up our hands?

What we must do is pitch in. But often old methods no

longer work. Therefore, our schools must adapt themselves to the new patterns and the ever-changing needs of our youngsters. There is much our schools can and must do.

During School

During school hours, an atmosphere of acceptance and respect must be fostered not only among the administration and leadership, but also among the faculty, students, and the rest of the school personnel, including the cafeteria and maintenance staff.

In quite a few schools the old medieval "fiefdom" atmosphere still prevails, where administrators are petty, puffed-up potentates who try to keep everyone else from encroaching on their turf. That attitude filters down, and some teachers act as if they are the upper crust. If they teach the talented kids, they relegate those of their colleagues who teach the "dumber" kids to the lower echelons. In turn, the less respected teachers frown on the teacher aides, who distance themselves from the lunchroom workers. They look askance at the janitorial staff. Therefore, the infrastructure of the whole school is one of prejudice and various levels of pseudo-superiority.

Naturally, this separatist attitude also permeates the student body. As soon as the students arrive, they find themselves nicknamed the Preps, Nerds, Jocks, Dorks, Rednecks.... The kids in the advanced placement classes call themselves the Brains or something similar. Other kids, feeling left out, might call themselves the Trenchcoat Mafia.

But whatever the naming and deriding process, kids learn their cliquishness from the adults who are prominent in their lives—the teachers and principals.

So it's with us that change must begin. All school staff—from the most brilliant "gifted class" teacher to the man or woman who sweeps the basement—need to interact more with each other. Unless adults set an example, kids won't learn to cooperate and not resort to name-calling. Teachers' lounges should be inclusive. Principals should be accessible, and a give-and-take atmosphere should prevail. Several times a year, teachers should switch classes, so that all faculty can appreciate the difficulty of various teaching assignments. And for a day or two, principals should assume the duties of the lunch line server, the attendance counselor, or the man or woman scrubbing toilet bowls. Kids should learn from the moment they step into school that people are different yet all are valuable, and that name-calling or making snide remarks about someone less swift, less fortunate, less wealthy, less handsome, or in an ethnic minority will not be tolerated.

After School

After-school programs need to be expanded everywhere, since many youngsters have no one to come home to. And healthy after-school refreshments should be available for kids who get hungry and need fortification.

Study halls and quiet homework time should be set aside as well, monitored by teachers who can patiently guide youngsters through their assignments. Many schools use after-school "detention" as a form of punishment for kids who skip school or are tardy. But what's needed is a spiffy, non-punitive homework center, set up in the cafeteria, for example, so kids can get their homework done before they get home.

At the same time, after-hours academic classes and work-shops should be offered. These classes shouldn't only provide accelerated courses but also makeup or remedial work. That way, students can improve their school skills dramatically or pick up new or higher level subjects that don't fit into their regular schedule.

Furthermore, training and coaching in the arts, computers and athletics should be on tap free of charge after school. Kids who are encouraged to use their talents—and every child has a talent—are too involved with their painting, dramatics, voice, or sculpture lessons to get into trouble. Also various sports not offered regularly should be made available, such as instruction in karate or boxing. Ballet classes and aerobic workouts could also be available.

After a survey, all kinds of exciting after-school presentations could be arranged so that any kid who wants to stay after school will have her time overflowing with productive activities. Jogging on a treadmill and getting involved in aerobics, charcoal sketching, and oratory would highlight the talents of all young-sters, not their troublemaking traits.

As a consequence, the ethnic barriers between the kids would crumble in no time. Kids are fair. Once they see how talented all their peers are, they will be impressed.

Of course, school buses would have to make two afternoon runs, one at 3:00 P.M. and another at 7:00 P.M. But the cost of those extra runs would soon be offset by the savings accumulated by the decrease in juvenile delinquency and youth violence.

Kids whose potential is highlighted don't become haters. And they don't become Hitlers.

On Weekends

Weekend academies and conferences also need to be established. Why should schools stand empty every Saturday and Sunday? Why not hold classes on weekend days too? Of course, attendance should be voluntary. Teachers would just teach whoever showed up—whole families, if need be. The faculty could rotate the weekend duties—most teachers would gladly teach one extra day a month, since their salaries always need a boost. Or staffs from other schools could come in. Or community leaders, from the sheriff to the mayor to the president of the bank to the owner of the automobile dealership and the garbage collectors' representative, could become guest lecturers or workshop presenters.

In this manner, society would become a learning mosaic, and the fear and suspicion that now exist among the various segments of our multicultural population would abate.

Evenings could see interdenominational talks of all kinds or readings of ancient texts in various languages. The fact is, our classrooms are underused, and if discussions dealing with faith were regularly held in classrooms and hallways, kids would have more respect for their schools. Of course, values-oriented meetings would also be voluntary. But why post the Ten Commandments in classrooms when it would be so much easier to hold discussions on faith, responsibility, and unselfishness in schools?

We must instill character in our young, so that their craving for hate and violence will lessen. Kids can only hold so much. Let's fill them up with goodness, so that evil is crowded out.

Summers and Vacations

Similarly, our schools should remain open throughout vacations and holidays. We have fine buildings, air-conditioned and heated in most cases. We have hordes of lost youngsters roaming the streets, not knowing what to do and looking to get into trouble. But if we keep schools open all year, there will always be a learning center to go to, a class to attend, a physical fitness program to check out, a free lesson in tennis or golf to take in, and an exciting pick-up game in the gym just waiting for our kids.

Schools in operation for only a certain number of days was a good idea back when kids were needed to work on the farms, or when families depended on other labor of their offspring. Today parents often work fifty-plus hours a week, when we include the commute. Then they have other meetings and obligations. What they need now is for our schools to step in and take up the supervisory roles Mom and Dad can no longer carry out to the extent that they used to.

It's not that today's parents are slack. Today's economy demands that they work themselves to the bone.

The Internet

Finally, schools must network not only regionally but nationally and globally to be on the forefront of information, and implement the techniques that work best. These days that's easy with the touch of a few computer keys. A national cutting-edge education center must be established to collect and synthesize programs that show promise. Then with one click of the mouse those best practices can be accessed by all schools in our nation.

Why should a school in Alaska not share its success stories with one in Florida? And why not right now?

Trust me. It will happen, just as soon as a widely publicized collection center is off and running. Then every morning, the first thing a school leader will do is check for the latest updates. Many people now spend their free seconds logging on to hot stock tips and getting excited about the newest commerce trends. But it's our kids' welfare we should be most excited about. Therefore, a practical scholastic skill hub that daily gathers the best methods being developed everywhere is an absolute necessity. For education should never stand still, just as our young never stand still. We adults must constantly learn new tactics and tacks—especially those that take the possibilities for potential violence out of our young.

Universal Preschools

One such new tack now being tried is a universal preschool program that would fling open the gates of public education to all kids ages three and up. No longer would parents have to scramble for affordable quality child care. They could send their three-year-olds off to school to learn pre-academic skills and have opportunities for artistic expression. Little kids could also make friends with other ethnic groups early on, so in later years it won't matter if their classmates are black, white, Hispanic, Asian, or Jewish.

This trend is certainly worth investigating. It would do much to steer our kids on the right academic path and remove many of their tendencies to go the violence route.

Parents' Support of Schools

Dedicated educators alone, however, can't do all that needs doing in our schools. Parents and other community members also need to get involved. The process begins with parents, who need to be encouraged to take an interest in what's going on at their child's school.

That goes not only for moms and dads who stay at home but for all parents. To get started, call the school and ask to speak to the person in charge of coordinating volunteers. That may be a teacher, a secretary, or most likely a PTA member.

Then get in touch with that coordinator. Explain how much time you can give each week, maybe just two hours to start, and what you're leaning toward. Do you want to help with the media center or the math tutoring? Or in the office or cafeteria? Or the sick room, the computer lab? With the annual candy sale, or the band boosters?

Even better, call your child's teacher and tell him you're eager to help with whatever projects are on the agenda. Most teachers will almost faint from joy over such an offer; they all have a long list of things a parent can do, even after hours when filing still needs to be done, folders need checking, notes have to be written.

Even if a parent is pressed for time, she can become a volunteer without interrupting her own work schedule. How? Call Kevin's teacher. Explain the dilemma: That you'd like to help out with field trips, reading groups, math circles, or essay contests but don't have a free minute. Then ask for the teacher's classroom wish list.

If she doesn't have one, compile your own. Kevin has come home complaining about how the dictionaries are falling apart, or that the book collection is a joke. Not to mention the prehistoric maps and lame educational toys. But those cost money, and money is scarce in schools.

That's where you come in: Write a check, attach a note stating the purpose of the check, and mail both to the office in care of the teacher. Repeat the process two or three times a year, then lounge in your cozy recliner and watch the results.

Your kids will be so proud of you and your support of their studies. Just imagine them reaching for a new mystery novel you bought or using some educational software you sponsored. You're also encouraging your children to study harder if they know your hard-earned money went for the new materials.

But what if you don't have the cash for those extras?

Then follow another plan. That is, volunteer on your own time after school without ever leaving the house. Do your volunteering via e-mail. Now you can become a teacher's right arm with only the click of your mouse. You can prepare for upcoming units, download information on those topics, and forward them to school. You can use the Internet to tutor your child's classmate who has been sick. You can take over as communication station for all parents in Crystal's class or for just a few. You can edit a PTA newsletter or make just one phone call per night reminding other parents of upcoming events. Point out that major tests are on the horizon. Would they please make sure their kids study hard, as you'll make sure yours will?

There are many small gestures you can make to support the schools in your community. You don't have to do it all by yourself, but you have to do your part.

Assessing Kids' Violence Potential at School

Unfortunately, however, not all kids are raised by caring, involved parents. They aren't looked after by other concerned adults or a close community either. That's why all schools across the nation must now assess the violence potential in their school population. And parents must be notified that from this moment on, no more youth violence is acceptable. None.

So, starting as early as fifth grade, all students must be given the following TEST (Tough Educational Safety Tactics) every year at the beginning of school. For the current students, the time is right now, and there's no time to lose.

The TEST can be printed on different colored papers—for example, on white paper for fifth grade, yellow for sixth grade, tan for seventh, gray for eighth, beige for ninth, orange for tenth, light green for eleventh, and light blue for twelfth grade—to make its administration easier.

Here it is.

TEST

Tough Educational Safety Tactics

Goal: To make sure there will be no more school violence

Students, please answer the following questions honestly. Answer Yes or No. You can print Yes or No, or you can just use Y or N. Do not write your name anywhere on this sheet, nor your teacher's name, your homeroom number, nor any other information, so no one will ever be able to know what your answers were.

1. Is it impossible for you to talk to your parent(s) or other adults?

2. Are you often upset, or do you get picked on a lot?

3. Can you get hold of a gun or other weapon if you want to?

4. Do you hate school and/or your teachers?

5. Do your friends try to get you to smoke, drink, take drugs, or participate in sex?

6. Do you have lots of free time?

7. Do you like people like Hitler, serial killers, or murderers?

8. Do you often wish you were dead?

When you are finished, fold your TEST and hand it to the administrator or teacher. And thank you for your honesty!

After the TEST has been given to students, administrators should tally the results. (If preferred, computer-compatible test sheets are available and can be scanned in seconds.) But no matter what format is used, in this self-reporting type of TEST, each Yes indicates a potential for youth violence.

Thus, after reviewing the results, principals and teachers will know exactly where to begin the process of redirecting their kids away from violence-prone behaviors to safety-conscious and healthy conduct. And the different colored sheets will help to target solutions directly to the grade levels that need them most.

If, for instance, many fifth-graders answer Yes to question #1, the PTA can sponsor parent workshops on better communications with their kids for those grade parents.

Should the sixth-graders give many Yes answers on question #2, counseling professionals can hold workshops dealing with feelings and how to honor all ethnic groups, thus eliminating name-calling and ridiculing.

If the seventh-graders overwhelmingly say Yes to question #3, speakers from the police department can address them and their parents, and teach them safety measures for guns in their possession. Gun locks must be issued and safety workshops held.

If the eighth-graders provide many Yes answers for question #4, a special effort must be made by their teachers to spice up lessons, tutor the kids, include them in field trips and fascinating school projects, bolster their attendance, and keep an eye on anyone failing at that grade level.

If many ninth-graders say Yes to question #5, schools can hold discussions and workshops on how to choose positive friends, how to say no to bad advice from friends, and teach the dangers of smoking, drinking, drugs, and premature sexual involvement.

If a large number of tenth-graders responds Yes to question #6, many high-interest after-school activities must be initiated, including sports, talent exploration, and positive computer projects. Opportunities for part-time work should be included.

If numerous eleventh-graders say Yes to question #7, a variety of "real" heroes must be introduced to the student body. Tiger Woods or another internationally known figure might give a guest lecture, lead an assembly, or be featured on posters and exhibits throughout eleventh-grade classrooms. Also literature dealing with heroic men and women can be read in English classes, and assignments can revolve around finding true heroes in the community.

Finally, if many twelfth-graders answer Yes to question #8, academic advisers must connect with them, hold orientation lessons for the future, invite reps from colleges and universities, let students attend a day on campus on a trial basis, arrange for shadowing opportunities (have students follow around a professional at work), institute flexible class scheduling, and invite dynamic, hope-giving speakers to encourage those youngsters. Not a single suicidal kid must be overlooked. Not one.

Of course, signals pointing toward violence won't fall neatly into grade levels. That is, Yes answers may come in clusters and may follow the lines of certain questions, rather than along chronological patterns. And TEST results may vary from year to year.

In that case, grade levels can be combined for workshops. Assemblies can be school-wide; real heroes can be invited for anyone interested. All parents might need to be informed about better communication with their kids. All teachers can rev up their skills.

And our country can finally unite in the war on violence!

But each of the questions in the TEST needs to be posed and the results examined. Here is another way of looking at them. These are the eight factors that determine the degree of violence potential in our youth:

1. The Family Factor (Key: Are parents and kids connected?)

2. The Emotion Factor (Key: Are kids constantly upset or picked on?)

3. The Weapon Factor (Key: Can kids get guns or other weapons easily?)

4. The School Factor (Key: Do kids like school?)

5. The Friend Factor (Key: What kinds of friends do kids have?)

6. The Free-Time Factor (Key: How do kids spend their free time?)

7. The Hero Factor (Key: Whom do kids admire?)

8. The Future Factor (Key: Do kids have plans for when they're grown?)

While this list of factors is not scientific, it gives each of us, educators and parents alike, a quick method to assess the violence potential of our youth. Moreover, it's intended to make all of us think and to ensure that all our nation's kids are taken care of. That means kids are bonded with their families, are not constantly upset or being called names, have zero access to weapons, enjoy their school, have nice friends, have meaningful things to do, have real heroes, and have a plan for their futures. Is that asking too much? No, it isn't.

This list and process don't demonize our kids; they exist for the children's benefit. And it's not profiling them either. Profiling is usually used only after the fact: police profile a killer after he or she has killed. That is, they make of list of characteristics that might fit someone who has already committed that crime or similar ones. Let's say no to profiling our youth.

But what I advocate is violence *proofing* our kids, and we can do it. If kids are assisted, if parents are helped in doing their part, and if schools are encouraged, urged—no, required—to test each of their kids for violence-prone indicators, then solutions can be found. We don't want to ever have to spring into action again after the fact.

Remember when you were in school and read *Our Town* by Thornton Wilder? And how the main character in this play, Emily, who died young, gets a chance to come back to life for one day? And how she loves it—she loves life? Oh, most of all she loves the simple things, "clocks ticking ... sunflowers ... food and coffee ... new-ironed dresses and hot baths and sleeping and waking up—Oh earth, you're too wonderful for anybody to realize...."

In that play Emily does get her chance to come back, but the poor kids killed in the Columbine massacre do not. Don't you fervently wish they could? Don't you wish that Dylan Klebold and Eric Harris could step back in time to the day before the horrific mass killings? So we could help them and halt the tragic events that were to come?

But the Columbine kids and their teacher are gone forever, as are the victims of all the other school shootings. And we don't know what great things they could have accomplished had they lived. How many of them were geniuses? How many were future Eleanor Roosevelts? Bill Gateses? Oprahs? How many would have helped the whole world? Hugged the whole world? Healed the whole world?

The fact is, we don't know what they might have done.

Yet they aren't truly gone if you wake up. Give a copy of the Eight Warning Signs of Youth Violence to all the parents you know, all teachers and other education-related workers, babysitters, youth workers, scout personnel, church, synagogue, and community leaders, police and welfare departments, grandparents and counselors, shopping mall administrators and neighbors of families with kids—in short, to anyone who ever comes in contact with a youngster.

That means all of us.

Just as we hang up the warning signs of cancer or reminders for women to give themselves breast exams, as we post calendars denoting upcoming events in our lives, as we save TV schedules, so must we now stick the Youth Violence Warning Signs on our refrigerators. So must we attach them to our laptop covers.

Only then can we rest assured that we have done what we can to make certain there won't ever be another school shooting. Only then can our dear Crystals and Kevins, and all our wonderful youngsters, be kids again, just ordinary, nice, fun-loving kids, who have much to look forward to.

Not one single kid should be allowed to go down the drain.

The fact that we're parents and grandparents, child care givers and teachers, friends and neighbors, church and synagogue leaders, coaches and youth workers, community and political leaders—the fact that we're alive and that we care!—at this pivotal time in history means we have within us the capacity to get the job done.

We can make a difference.

The Eight Signs of Being Violence-Proofed

Wouldn't it be a catastrophe if the United States would implode like a roach-infested high-rise tenement targeted for demolition just because we adults didn't care enough about our kids to make them safe?

But I believe we do care. That's why I implore you to check up on every kid you come into contact with. Stop whatever you're doing and examine each and every youngster in your home, family, kindergarten or play group, classroom, school, neighborhood, church, synagogue, and on the teams you coach. In your mind, examine them to see if they're immune to youth violence.

Are they all violence-proofed? To make sure, think about all those kids now, and ask yourself the following questions about each one (answer Yes or No):

1. Does this kid listen to, or confide in, a parent or other family member or adult?

2. When this kid gets depressed or angry over a broken friendship, ridicule, or alienation by peers, does he or she bounce back?

3. Does this kid have *no* access to guns or other weapons? And is this kid *not* fascinated by guns, other weapons, or fire?

4. Are this kid's grades, interest in school, and attendance good or rising?

5. Are this kid's friends a positive influence and not encouraging him or her to smoke, drink, do drugs, or have sex?

6. Is this kid involved in church or synagogue, athletics, positive clubs and hobbies, volunteering, or work?

7. Does this kid idolize real heroes (good role models)? Is this kid *not* fascinated by violent games, movies, music, or Internet sites? Is he or she *not* cruel?

8. Does this kid have a future success plan and feel life is worthwhile?

If you have answered Yes to all statements, be glad. But even if you haven't, now you know what must be done. So please, get busy. The safety and well-being of the kids and the whole community may be at stake.

Support Systems and Organizations

The Pacific Center for Violence Prevention

http://www.pcvp.org/

A project of the Trauma Foundation, works to prevent youth violence in California. Located at San Francisco General Hospital, the Center serves as the policy headquarters for the Violence Prevention Initiative funded by the California Wellness Foundation.

Youth Crime Watch

http://www.ycwa.org/

Relies on the principle of citizenship; youths take an active role in addressing the problems around them. Once youths and youth advisors are trained in Youth Crime Watch methods, these youngsters take ownership of their own Youth Crime Watch program for their school, neighborhood, public housing site, recreational center, or park. Youth Crime Watch enables youths to participate actively in reducing crime and drug use in their schools and communities.

Teen Help Adolescent Resources

http://vpp.com/teenhelp/

Offers support for families with teen challenges, and provides a national toll-free hotline to assist parents, child care professionals, and others in locating appropriate resources for the treatment of adolescents struggling with making the best choices in their lives.

If you would like to learn how Teen Help can help your son or daughter, please call 1-800-840-5704.

The New York University Child Study Center

http://aboutourkids.org/

A multidisciplinary team of professionals dedicated to advancing the field of mental health for children and their families through evidence-based practice, science, and education. The center offers expert psychiatric services for children and families, with emphasis on early diagnosis and intervention. The center integrates the finest research with patient care and state-of-the-art training, utilizing an extraordinary new facility and the resources of the world-class NYU School of Medicine. Program specialists translate scientific developments and innovative procedures into everyday techniques for parents, educators, pediatricians, and other mental health professionals. The Center's vision is to be the premiere source of child mental health information by improving and influencing the practice of child mental health professionals and, in so doing, change the face of children's mental health in this country.

"You're the One Who Can Make the Peace"

http://www.angelfire.com/mn/makethepeace/index.html

Campaign mission statement is, "To promote peace through a community-wide awareness and education initiative that recognizes each individual as the one to make the peace."

This new initiative by the Citizens and Youth Violence Intervention Council (CYVIC) for Rochester, Minnesota, and the surrounding communities, in conjunction with the Diversity Council and the Mayor's Community Response Team, strives to build on the recent success and foundation established by the "Not in Our Town" campaign. The new Make the Peace Campaign will involve a proactive and positive theme that promotes peaceful actions, positive solutions, and individual recognition in a climate of peace and hope.

For more information please write: CYVIC (Citizens and Youth Violence Intervention Council), 615 7th Street SW, Rochester, MN 55902, or call Dottie Hecht at 507-289-1649. Or e-mail us at faces@infonet.isl.net. We all have an opportunity and obligation to be involved in helping make our community a more peaceful environment for all.

"You're the One Who Can Make the Peace" is a statewide initiative of the Minnesota Department of Children, Families, and Learning, Office of Drug Policy and Violence Prevention.

Treatment Centers—available through pavnet

(affiliated with the criminal justice system)

Abraxas Group, Inc.

http://www.reeusda.gov/pavnet/pm/pmabrax.htm

Contact: Arlene Lissner, President

Abraxas Group, Inc.
2300 Two PNC Plaza
620 Liberty Avenue
Pittsburgh, PA 15222
Tel: 412-562-0105, 800-ABRAXAS
Fax: 412-562-9408

Targets juvenile delinquents, victims of abuse, and youths diagnosed with mental health problems. It has locations in Milford, Delaware; Shelby, Ohio; Bethlehem, Erie, Harrisburg, Marienville, Philadelphia, Pittsburgh, Pittston, and South Mountain, Pennsylvania; and Washington, D.C., and has been cited by the Office of Juvenile Justice and Delinquency Prevention (OJJDP) and by the Alcohol, Drug Abuse, and Mental Health Administration as a national model in the treatment of high-risk youth, and received numerous awards at the national, state, and local levels.

Services include screening and assessment; counseling; education programs; substance abuse treatment; campus and community-based intensive residential treatment; boot camps; residential special needs programs for sex offenders, adolescent females, drug sellers, youths with mental health problems, and youths with emotional and behavioral disorders; transitional care residences; day treatment programs; and supervised independent living programs.

Assessment, Intervention, and Transition (AIT) Program

http://www.co.multnomah.or.us/dcj/jcjaitp.htm

Contact: Thuy Vanderlinde, Program Administrator

Multnomah County Department of Juvenile Justice Services
Assessment, Intervention, and Transition Program
1401 N.E. 68th Avenue
Portland, OR 97213
Tel: 503-988-3460
Fax: 503-988-3218
TTD: 503-988-3561

Targets male and female gang members and other at-risk youth ages thirteen to eighteen. Referrals must be failing in traditional probation services in the community. It is a residential treatment facility at the Department of Juvenile Justice Services Complex in Multnomah County, Portland, Oregon.

Services include a thirty-day program that has three components: assessment, intervention, and transition. Youths receive continual multidisciplinary assessments by interactive program staff who rely heavily on group participation and family meetings to gather information rather than traditional "interview-oriented" assessment modalities. AIT intervention incorporates four treatment models: the cognitive restructuring skill-building model, the behavior model, the relationship model, and the positive peer culture model.

Bethesda Day Treatment Center, Inc.

http://www.reeusda.gov/pavnet/yt/Ytbethct.htm

Contact: Jerilyn Keen, Managing Director

Bethesda Day Treatment Center, Inc.
P. O. Box 270
Central Oak Heights
West Milton, PA 17886-0270
Tel: 717-568-1131
Fax: 717-568-1134

Targets delinquent juvenile offenders, ages ten to eighteen, and has a treatment center that serves the city of Philadelphia, Pennsylvania, and eleven counties in the state of Pennsylvania.

Services include the provision of life skills and career opportunities as well as a variety of counseling approaches (group, family, and individual) and values-oriented treatments to help facilitate social reintegration. Operating during nontraditional hours, including weekends and evenings, the program also offers an individualized educational program, drug and alcohol abuse counseling, foster care, and outpatient family systems counseling.

For additional information contact:

Dominic Herbst, President

Bethesda Day Treatment Center, Inc.

Boys Town/Father Flanagan's Boys' Home

http://www.reeusda.gov/pavnet/yt/Ytboysto.htm

Contact: Randy Blauvelt, Director of Public Relations

Boys Town/Father Flanagan's Boys' Home
14100 Crawford Street
Boys Town, NE 68010
Tel: 402-498-1300
Fax: 402-498-1348
E-mail: helpkids@boystown.org or blauvelr@boystown.org
Web address: http://www.boystown.org

Targets abused and disadvantaged youth, and offers residential and treatment facilities and programs nationwide, and career skills training in Omaha, Nebraska.

Services include a multitude of programs for abused and troubled youth, such as emergency shelter services that provide short-term care for runaway and troubled youth ages ten to eighteen; family preservation services that offer intensive in-home treatment for families in crisis; treatment foster family services that allow trained parents to provide supportive and nurturing environments to children; family-style care and treatment homes for abused, abandoned, neglected, or otherwise troubled children; a training program that teaches parents how to deal more effectively with their children.

Also, the Boys Town National Hotline, 1-800-448-3000, is a full-service crisis, resource, and referral service that handles all kinds of problems; a reading center that conducts research on literacy education of youths at the middle school and high school levels; and a national resource and training center that provides training and program development services to other youth care agencies, schools, and psychiatric hospitals.

Capital Offender Program

http://www.reeusda.gov/pavnet/yt/Ytcapita.htm

Contact: Linda Reyes, Ph.D., Assistant Deputy Executive Director

Rehabilitation Services
Texas Youth Commission
4900 North Lamar
P. O. Box 4260
Austin, TX 78765
Tel: 512-424-6152

Targets youths incarcerated for homicide. Its location is the Giddings State Home and School, Giddings, Texas.

Services include an intensive, sixteen-week, offense-specific group treatment program for juveniles who have been committed for homicide. A group of eight juveniles lives together and meets twice per week for approximately three hours per session. Role playing is a key element of the group sessions; additionally, participants role-play the homicide for which they were committed. In the re-enactment, the youth first plays himself and then the victim.

Chatham-Savannah Youth Futures Authority

http://www.reeusda.gov/pavnet/yt/Ytchatsa.htm

Contact: Dr. Otis Johnson, Executive Director

Chatham-Savannah Youth Futures Authority
316 East Bay Street
Savannah, GA 31401
Tel: 912-651-6810
Fax: 912-651-6814

Targets children and at-risk youths and their families, primarily those who have low incomes. Its location is the middle schools in Chatham County and Savannah, Georgia, St. Pius X Family Resource Center, and churches.

Services include the screening of all students at four middle schools. Those identified as at risk receive intensive services by multidisciplinary "Stay Teams." In addition, a Teenage Parenting Program is offered, in which pregnant teenagers may leave their home schools and attend an alternative school. Furthermore, in a Comprehensive Competencies Program, the grade level for each middle school student is diagnosed by computer, and students behind by at least two grades receive a personalized program designed to bring them up to their appropriate grade levels. For students promoted to high school, a Transition Resource Teacher provides a link between the home, school, and community agencies that provide needed services.

Also in operation are several preschool education centers with a teacher, paraprofessional, and family advocate to help families get needed services; the Burger King Academy, funded by Burger King and other local sources, to provide an alternative educational setting for those who respond better to nontraditional approaches; a Family Resource Center, which offers a wide array of family-based services and activities directed by neighborhood residents in a targeted area of the city; and the Black Male Task Force, formed to address the special needs of male African American students.

Child Witness to Violence Project (CWVP)

http://www.reeusda.gov/pavnet/yt/ytcwvp.htm

Contact: Betsy McAlister Groves, LICSW, Project Director

Child Witness to Violence Project
Boston Medical Center
818 Harrison Avenue, T214
Boston, MA 02118
Tel: 617-414-4244
Fax: 617-414-7915
E-mail: Betsy.Groves@BMC.org
Web address:
http://www.bostonchildhealth.org/ChildWitnesstoViolence/index.htm

Targets children age eight or younger who have witnessed violence. It is set in Boston, Massachusetts, and was a finalist for a 1996 Innovations in American Government Award sponsored by the Ford Foundation and the Kennedy School of Government at Harvard University.

Services include counseling and advocacy, with emphasis on rapid response and intervention, to young children who have witnessed violence, stabilizing the child's environment (school, day care, and home), and consulting with families and others who interact with the child on a regular basis. Educational and outreach services with numerous components are also provided.

Choice Program

http://www.reeusda.gov/pavnet/yt/Ytchoice.htm

Contact: Dr. John S. Martello, Executive Director

The Shriver Center at UMBC
1000 Hilltop Circle
Baltimore, MD 21250
Tel: 410-455-2494
Fax: 410-455-1074

Targets minor and status juvenile offenders, and is set in homes and communities in the Baltimore, Maryland, and Washington, D.C., areas. Services include an intensive monitoring, treatment, and multiple-service approach that is home-based and family-oriented. The program is unique because of the intensity of contact between its caseworkers and clients—three to five contacts per day are required during the initial stages—and in the limits placed on length of service for caseworkers to avoid burnout.

Caseworkers are generally recent college graduates. They meet regularly with family members and school personnel, and may call on outside expertise (for example, psychologists, substance abuse counselors) as necessary. The close and intensive daily contact allows for careful tracking of the client's progress.

For additional information contact:

Craig Dempsey, Director

The Choice Program
University of Maryland at Baltimore County
1000 Hilltop Circle
Baltimore, MD 21250

Comin' Up

http:www.reeusda.gov/pavnet/yt/Ytcomnup.htm

Contact: Richard Zavala, Director

Parks and Community Services Department
4200 South Freeway, Suite 2200
Fort Worth, TX 76115-1499
Tel: 817-871-5711
Fax: 817-871-5724

Targets gang-involved youths and operates in six community centers and two Boys and Girls Clubs in Fort Worth, Texas.

Services include need-based service plans and activities tailored to each individual youth. A service plan involves a two-step educational process, usually starting with basic life skills such as communication and conflict resolution. The second phase addresses more complex issues, including academic and job development, peer mediation, and substance abuse counseling. Progress is monitored by a team of project staff; school, police, and probation officials; and parents. Interest-based activities, including sports events, music and drama programs, and field trips, support the service plans.

Detained Adolescent Dad Support (DADS)

http://www.reeusda.gov/pavnet/yt/ytdetado.htm

Contact: Scott Haberman, Deputy Probation Officer

Los Angeles County Probation Department
Camp Karl Holton
12653 North Little Tujunga Canyon Road
San Fernando, CA 91342
Tel: 818-896-0571
Fax: 818-896-9239

Targets male minors in the criminal justice system in Los Angeles County, California, operates in Camp Karl Holton juvenile correctional facility, San Fernando, California, and was recognized by the National Association of Counties, the organization that represents county governments in the United States, with a 1995 Achievement Award.

Services include twelve-session orientations for male minors covering parenting skills, sex education, sex roles, self-esteem, and the importance of responsibility for young fathers. Probation officers or teachers refer students to the program. Other students may also choose to attend.

For additional information, contact:

Bill Fenton, Director, Camp Karl Holton, and Probation Director, Los Angeles County

Edwin Gould Academy's Unified Approach to Foster Care

http://www.reeusda.gov/pavnet/yt/ytgould.htm

Contact: Thomas Webber, Superintendent/Executive Director

Edwin Gould Academy
Ramapo Union Free School District
675 Chestnut Ridge Road
Chestnut Ridge, NY 10977-6222
Tel: 914-573-5920
Fax: 914-578-5697
E-mail: webberega@compuserve.com

Targets youth ages twelve to twenty-one and offers integrated foster care. Its setting is north of Manhattan in Chestnut Ridge, New York. It has won a 1998 Innovations in American Government Award sponsored by the Ford Foundation and the Kennedy School of Government at Harvard University.

Services are based on a Unified Approach to Foster Care, with the goal of maximizing fund allocation through the centralization of management activities. The academy is nondepartmental; one person is responsible for training and supervision of the faculty. Thus, service providers (teachers, psychologists, social workers, child care workers, health care providers, and school and residential administrators) are trained to provide for each child in the same manner. Furthermore, personnel at every level participate in the group decision making process. Preparation for postsecondary schooling, school-to-work programs, and extended continuing care services are also offered.

EMPOWER I and II

http://www.reeusda.gov/pavnet/yt/Ytempowe.htm

Contact: Jill Watson

The Founders School
106 River Road
East Haddam, CT 06423
Tel: 203-873-1480

Targets at-risk male youth under jurisdiction of the Department of Children and Youth Services and is set in Founders School, a private residential facility in East Haddam, Connecticut.

Services include a full educational program and support services designed to return its students to mainstream society. The EMPOWER I program operates during the summer. Participants who do well move into the EMPOWER II program during the regular school year. The programs provide on-campus career development sites.

A unique feature of the curriculum is the opportunity provided to selected participants to put their training to use in a hands-on boat-building project which connects academic skills with practical employment skills, incorporating math and reading instruction with carpentry training. Students learn how to read and use design plans and blueprints by constructing a sailboat, which provides tangible proof of skills acquired.

Gang Related Intervention Program (GRIP)

http://www.reeusda.gov/pavnet/yt/Ytgangre.htm

Contact: Jacolyn Levin, Assistant Commissioner

Westchester County Probation Department
112 East Post Road, Third Floor
White Plains, NY 10601
Tel: 914-285-3569
Fax: 914-285-3507
E-mail: JGL1@ofs.co.westchester.ny.us

Targets probationers between ages fourteen and twenty-one who are involved in gang activity or are at risk for gang involvement. Its setting is Mount Vernon, New York. It was recognized by the National Association of Counties, the organization that represents county governments in the U.S., with a 1995 Achievement Award.

Services include programs geared toward providing opportunities for participants to learn to live productive, crime-free lives; the program utilizes therapeutic and cognitive life skill groups to promote change in socially unacceptable attitudes and behaviors. Priority is given to youth who are either involved in gang activity or are at risk of gang involvement, are substance abusers, or are prone to violence. Target youth share many characteristics, such as neglect or loss of parental control, low self-esteem, family history of gang involvement, truancy, or poor school performance, weapons use, violent behavior, prior arrests, drug use, and drug dealing.

Harper Alternative School

http:www.reeusda.gov/pavnet/yt/ytharper.htm

Contact: Steve D. Allen, Special Education Director,
Alternative District

Houston Independent School District
3830 Richmond Avenue
Houston, TX 77027
Tel: 713-892-6100
Fax: 713-892-6109
E-mail: SteveHoust@aol.com

Targets students who bring illegal weapons onto a Houston Independent School District campus. Its setting is Harper Alternative School, Houston, Texas. An evaluation by the Research Department of the Houston Independent School District conducted in 1992–1993 found a zero percent recidivism rate among students who went through the program.

Services include the assignment of suitable students to Harper Alternative School for twelve weeks. During this time, the students remain enrolled at their original schools, which provide the instructional materials that a Harper teacher uses for instruction. Students also receive counseling and, at the end of the twelve weeks, either return to their previous school or another one in the Houston Independent School District.

For additional information contact:

Bernie Callip, Harper Social Worker, or
Paul Hanser, Harper Executive Director
Tel: 713-802-4760

Kansas City as Schools (KCAS)

http://www.reeusda.gov/pavnet/yt/Ytkansas.htm

Contact: Pam Wiens, Director of Education and
Employment Training

Associated Youth Services
1620 South 27th Street
Box 6145
Kansas City, KS 66106
Tel: 913-831-2820
Fax: 913-831-0262

Targets juvenile offenders, ex-offenders, and at-risk youth ages thirteen
to twenty-one, and is offered by Associated Youth Services, a nonprofit
corporation with headquarters in the Argentine district of Kansas City,
Kansas. Begun in 1912 as a Mennonite orphanage and expanded in
the1970s, the program offers group homes for teenage boys.

Moreover, specialized foster care, substance abuse counseling,
alternative education, and employment training in Kansas City and
across Kansas are provided for youth who face multiple barriers to
graduating from high school and maintaining employment. In addition to being economically disadvantaged, school dropouts, or students at risk of dropping out, and having low academic skills, many
of the clients are juvenile offenders or ex-offenders, substance
abusers, or adolescent parents.

National Student Athlete Day

http://www.reeusda.gov/pavnet/yt/Ytnatstu.htm

Contact: Donn T. Davis

Department of Juvenile Justice
14375 Main Street, Suite 079M
Upper Marlboro, MD 20772
Tel: 301-952-2580
Fax: 301-952-2954

Targets juvenile offenders, operates at the University of Maryland,
College Park campus, and brings 150 juvenile offenders in the

Baltimore-Washington area together with student athletes at the University of Maryland for a day of activities stressing academic achievement and athletic competition. The athletes serve to guide the juveniles, who rotate among the six activity stations. By having the student athletes act as role models, juveniles can see firsthand how academics and sports can lead to an enriching school experience. Group discussions ensue during lunch, and an awards ceremony concludes the day.

The program is sponsored by the University of Maryland Criminology and Criminal Justice Alumni Chapter, Department of Criminology and Criminal Justice, Department of Intercollegiate Athletics, and the Academic Support for Returning Athletes Program. The Maryland Department of Juvenile Services supports and assists the program.

New Futures School

http://www.reeusda.gov/pavnet/yt/Ytnewfut.htm

Contact: Virginia Sisneros, Director of Day Care Services

New Futures School
5400 Cutler N.E.
Albuquerque, NM 87110
Tel: 505-883-5680
Fax: 505-880-3977

Targets pregnant adolescents and adolescent parents, operates in the alternative school (New Futures) in Albuquerque, New Mexico, and sends almost 75 percent of its graduates on to postsecondary education, while nationally fewer than half of adolescent parents graduate from high school.

Services include education, health, counseling, vocational training, and child care services for pregnant adolescents and adolescent parents. The program's mission is to help and motivate school-age parents to make informed decisions and help them complete their secondary education. It encourages them to have healthy pregnancies and become responsible parents.

There are four onsite child care facilities; volunteers include five foster grandparents. A jobs training program is available for thirty to forty students per year. The school has two departments, the Perinatal Program, in which a pregnant teenager remains for one or two semesters; and the Young Parents' Center for school-age mothers and fathers unable to successfully participate in regular school following the birth of their children.

Resocialization Program

http://www.reeusda.gov/pavnet/yt/Ytresocl.html

Contact: Linda S. Reyes, Ph.D., Assistant Deputy Executive Director, Rehabilitation Services

Texas Youth Commission
4900 North Lamar
P. O. Box 4260
Austin, TX 78765
Tel: 512-424-6152

Targets incarcerated youth and is set in Texas Youth Commission institutions, halfway houses, and Contract Care programs.

Services include a multimodal approach that combines a variety of interventions with emphasis on therapeutic community concepts and cognitive behavioral interventions in a continuum-of-care context. The major components are assessment, provision of a therapeutic environment, intervention to stop negative behavior, rehabilitation to promote positive behavior, and community reintegration. In this performance-based program, youth are required to demonstrate sufficient internal controls to maintain appropriate behavior in order to transition to less restrictive placements. Progress is measured through five identified phases using a Resocialization Phases Checklist.

Saturday Institute for Manhood, Brotherhood, Actualization (SIMBA)

http://www.reeusda.gov/pavnet/yt/Ytsatint.htm

Contact: David Reed, Director

SIMBA
Wholistic Stress Control Institute
3480 Greenbriar Parkway, Suite 310B
P. O. Box 42841
Atlanta, GA 30331
Tel: 404-344-2021
Fax: 404-349-1924

Targets incarcerated male African American youth and operates in a correctional facility in Georgia.

Services—aimed at reducing the high death rate of African American males due to violence, alcohol, other drug use, and poor health care—include twelve consecutive Saturday sessions in which African American history, vocational training, health education, and aesthetic arts are taught. Youths have been placed in jobs or in training as a result of the vocational development component. Some have also formed a speaker's bureau and appear at schools, meetings, and other places.

Second Chance Offender Program

http://www.reeusda.gov/pavnet/yt/Ytseccha.htm

Contact: Gary Johnson, JTPA Director

Second Chance Offender Program
JTPA, SDA 13
310 West Kanesville Boulevard
Room 101
Council Bluffs, IA 51503-0772
Tel: 712-322-4138
Fax: 712-322-5097

Targets juvenile offenders and is located in Council Bluffs, Iowa.

Services offer juvenile offenders the chance to turn their lives into a positive, productive direction. Jointly administered by Pottawattomie Juvenile Court Services and JTPA, the program provides youth with group activities, behavior modification classes, and pre-employment training. Parent classes are scheduled in conjunction with classes for youth. Older youth may also participate in a work experience activity.

Overall the goals of the program are to reduce recidivism, improve self-esteem and motivation, reinforce school-to-work concepts, open the lines of communication, and reinforce positive values. During evening group meetings, youths discuss such topics as alcohol, talking through disagreements, sexually transmitted diseases, and the cost of living.

For additional information contact:

John Sutton
Tel: 712-322-4138

Spectrum Wilderness Program

http://www.reeusda.gov/pavnet/yt/Ytspectr.htm

Contact: Tim Humes, Program Coordinator

Spectrum Wilderness Program
Southern Illinois University
Carbondale, IL 62901
Tel: 618-453-1121
Fax: 618-453-1188
E-mail: thumes@siu.edu

Targets delinquent and otherwise troubled youth. It begins in southern Illinois and, depending on weather conditions, continues in Arkansas, Georgia, Texas, Wyoming, Missouri, or Ontario, Canada.

Services include a thirty-day therapeutic outdoor program operated by the Touch of Nature Environmental Center at Southern Illinois University. Backpacking, canoeing, caving, team courses, rope courses, rock climbing, and community service projects are on the agenda. Students are involved in all daily chores for these programs, including making camp, cooking, and cleaning.

The program emphasizes academics as well, and has a strong group counseling component in which behavior problems are addressed and successes are recognized. A seventy-six-day course for older students (ages sixteen to eighteen) that focuses on independent living skills is also offered.

Total Competence System

http://www.reeusda.gov/pavnet/yt/Yttotcom.htm

Contact: Director

Total Competence System
Franklin Learning Systems
20 Ketchum Street
Westport, CT 06880
Tel: 800-999-0384

Targets youth and young adults needing education alternatives, particularly those adjudicated or incarcerated, and is located in Maryland.

Services include a series of programs with the Maryland Department of Juvenile Services to help prepare out-of-school youth and young adults for today's changing workplace. In developing the curriculum, research involved extensive interviews with youth and staff members (including educators, residential staff, counselors, and psychologists). The learning design stresses positive modeling of behavior, practice, and feedback. The courses are conducted orally, with most discussions in a classroom setting. As a result, students with learning disabilities, such as dyslexia, or students who are several grade levels below their age can profit from the program.

Transitional Aftercare Group (TAG) Program

http://www.reeusda.gov/pavnet/yt/Yttranaf.htm

Contact: John C. Smith, M.S.W.

Health Promotions
Morehouse School of Medicine
720 Westview Drive S.W.
Atlanta, GA 30310
Tel: 404-752-1754
Fax: 404-752-0094

Targets recently released juvenile offenders in the state of Georgia and offers aftercare group programs for juveniles making the transition from incarceration to community. Designed to reduce recidivism among newly released juvenile offenders, the program provides case management, treatment services, and career, educational, and vocational training.

Case management includes a needs assessment of each person, crisis intervention, treatment planning, referrals, and placement. Treatment services include counseling, parenting classes, alcohol abuse education, drug abuse education, success seminars, and literacy education. Career, educational, and vocational training includes basic skills and instruction related to receiving a high school diploma, career counseling, and job placement. Partners include the Morehouse School of Medicine and the Georgia Department of Children and Youth Services.

For additional information contact:

National Center for Injury Prevention and Control
Centers for Disease Control and Prevention
Division of Violence Prevention
Tel: 404-488-4646

Urban Interpersonal Violence Injury Control Project

http://www.reeusda.gov/pavnet/yt/Yturbani.htm

Contact: Ibrehim Mohammad, Coordinator for Project Redirect
Ad Hoc Group Against Crime

3330 Troost
Kansas City, MO 64109
Tel: 816-531-0000

Targets youth and adults who have shown a tendency to violent behavior. Set in Kansas City, Missouri, and conceived to address risk factors for homicide, the project was built on the results of a previous study of black-on-black homicide, commissioned by the Ad Hoc Group Against Crime. This study found that past assaultive behavior was a strong predictor of a person becoming a homicide victim or perpetrator.

Therefore, the project focuses on recruiting those who have shown a prior tendency for violence as targets for learning and developing conflict resolution skills, and on teaching participants how to avoid violent confrontations.

VisionQuest National, Ltd.

http://www.reeusda.gov/pavnet/yt/Ytvision.htm

Contact: Bob Burton, Chief Executive Officer

VisionQuest National, Ltd.
P. O. Box 12906
Tucson, AZ 85732
Tel: 602-881-3950

Targets juvenile offenders ages twelve to eighteen, and has locations in Arizona, California, Florida, Pennsylvania, Texas, and New Jersey. Evaluations by the RAND Corporation found the program produced substantially lower recidivism rates among its graduates. The Center for Juvenile Justice Training and Research and Arthur Young found that graduates were less likely to commit violent crimes than they were prior to the program.

This private national program serves as an alternative to incarceration for serious juvenile offenders who enter the program via juvenile courts, probation departments, and social service agencies. Youth deal with issues such as child abuse and abandonment, which have dominated their lives. Treatment plans last twelve to fifteen months and are tailored to meet each youth's specific physical, educational, psychological, and behavioral needs. Individualized treatment plans are constantly updated and include challenging outdoor activities and education plans.

The program sequence involves three months in an orientation wilderness camp; five months in an adventure program such as a wagon train or sailing expedition, which offers participants an alternative setting in which to learn cooperation and responsibility; and five months in a community residential program.

Other programs include HomeQuest (which serves as a bridge), Boot and Hat Camp (an intensive three-month program for young men facing their first out-of-home placement), and New Directions (which combines an alternative school, shelter, and comprehensive diagnostics center).

For additional information contact:

VisionQuest National, Ltd.
Eastern Regional Office
Tel: 610-458-0800, or
VisionQuest National, Ltd.
Dallas Operations
Tel: 214-631-3993

Weekend Challenge Program (WCP)

http://www.reeusda.gov/pavnet/yt/Ytweeken.htm

Contact: Philip Duket, Supervisor

Lutheran Social Services
5820 Third Avenue
Kenosha, WI 53140
Tel: 414-658-3154
Fax: 414-658-0841

Targets chronic juvenile offenders, ages twelve to seventeen, and is set outdoors in Kenosha, Wisconsin.

Services include outdoor activities to help chronic juvenile offenders improve their self-image. Canoeing, whitewater rafting, skiing, caving, and other outdoor pursuits encourage trust building, goal setting, problem solving, challenge through stress, and humor. As youths experience physical success, they focus on breaking the cycle of failure that causes a negative self-concept. Using self-imposed limits, they learn that only their best effort is acceptable in this highly structured and supportive framework.

Youth as Resources (Special Populations)

http://www.reeusda.gov/pavnet/yt/Ytyouspe.htm

Contact: Maria Nagorski, Deputy Executive Director

National Crime Prevention Council
1700 K Street N.W., Second Floor
Washington, DC 20006-3817
Tel: 202-466-6272, ext. 151

Targets youth in care. It is set in youth residential care and detention facilities nationwide. Evaluations have shown that youths involved benefit both as community members and as individuals by being able to demonstrate their positive competencies, and by being valued as useful members of the community.

Services include various youth projects that can be carried out within the care setting or at community locations, depending on the circumstances of the youths involved and on security considerations.

A local board that includes youths and adults solicits project applications from the youths and determines which ones will be funded. Staff at the care facilities generally serve as the adult project sponsors and mentors. They receive training in working in this partnership rather than supervisory relationship with youths in their charge. Youths and adults are trained in project design and implementation. Support for staff and youth efforts also comes from training provided to the administrative staffs of the agencies.

Recommended Reading

Bernall, Misty. *She Said Yes: The Unlikely Martyrdom of Cassie Bernall.* Farmington, PA: Plough 1999.

Blankenhorn, David. *Fatherless America: Confronting Our Most Urgent Social Problem.* New York: Basic, 1995.

Clinton, Hillary. *It Takes a Village: And Other Lessons Children Teach Us.* New York: Simon and Schuster, 1996.

Cloud, Robert C. *Solutions for Youth Violence for Schools and Communities: A Resource Guide.* Waco, TX: Health Edco, 1997.

De Becker, Gavin. *The Gift of Fear: And Other Survival Signals That Protect Us from Violence.* New York: Dell, 1997.

_____. De Becker, Gavin. *Protecting the Gift: Keeping Children and Teenagers Safe (and Parents Sane).* New York: Dial Press, 1999.

Flannery, Raymond B. *Preventing Youth Violence: A Guide for Parents, Teachers, and Counselors.* New York: Continuum, 1999.

Garbarino, James. *Lost Boys: Why Our Sons Turn Violent and How We Can Save Them.* New York: Free Press, 1999.

Gurian, Michael. *A Fine Young Man: What Parents, Mentors, and Educators Can Do to Shape Adolescent Boys into Exceptional Men.* New York: Putnam, 1998.

Kindlon, Daniel J., et al. *Raising Cain: Protecting the Emotional Life of Boys.* New York: Ballantine, 1999.

Loomans, Diane. *Full Esteem Ahead: 100 Ways to Build Self-Esteem in Children and Adults.* Tiburon, CA: HJ Kramer, 1994.

_____. *The Laughing Classroom: Everyones's Guide to Teaching With Humor and Play.* Tiburon, CA: HJ Kramer, 1993.

Mones, Paul. *When a Child Kills.* New York: Pocket, 1992.

Peck, M. Scott. *The Road Less Traveled: A New Psychology of Love, Traditional Values and Spiritual Growth*. New York: Simon and Schuster, 1993.

Pipher, Mary. *Reviving Ophelia: Saving the Selves of Adolescent Girls*. New York: Ballantine, 1995.

Snortland, Ellen. *Beauty Bites Beast: Awakening the Warrior Within Women and Girls*. Pasadena, CA: Trilogy Books, 1996.

Voices of Columbine: An Anthology by Students and Teachers of Columbine High School. Wakefield, RI: Moyer Bell, forthcoming.

Wooden, Kenneth. *Child Lures: What Every Parent and Child Should Know About Preventing Sexual Abuse and Abduction*. Arlington, TX: Summit Pulbishing Group, 1995.

Zimring, Franklin E. *American Youth Violence*. New York: Oxford University Press, 1998.

Helpful Internet Sites and Articles

Adolescent Health and Mental Health

http://www.fenichel.com/adolhealth.shtm

An Internet guide to adolescent mental health issues, including self-esteem, peer pressure, dating, and family stress. Links and interactive advice for parents and teens. (Fenichel)

The American Counseling Association Responds to School Violence

http://www.counseling.org/schoolviolence/

Professional counselors respond to school violence.

American School Counselor Association

http://www.schoolcounselor.org/

Review early warning signs, violence prevention resources, and counseling programs. Contains publications, services, highlights, and events.

Anger and Narcissistic Personalities

http://www.apa.org/releases/self.htm

A thoughtful (graduate- and professional-level) review of the relationship between humiliation and violent anger in the context of recent mass-shootings by children in public schools. Self-esteem vs. self-absorption. (APA)

Bullying

http://www.apa.org/monitor/oct99/cf3.htm

"Bullying widespread in middle school, say three studies" (APA Monitor, October 99)

Center for the Prevention of School Violence

http://www.ncsu.edu/cpsv

School violence, safe schools pyramid, special projects, public awareness campaign, newsletters, research bulletins, research briefs, etc.

Children and TV Violence

http://www.parenthoodweb.com/articles/phw247.htm

Discussion of both the numbing and imitative aspects of exposure to television violence. From AACAP's user-friendly Parenthood Web.

Children and Violence

http://www.apa.org/concept/children.html#violence

From the APA's collection of articles on children's issues. (See also Children and Television Violence)

Committee for Children

http://www.cfchildren.org/

Provides anti-violence and child abuse curricula for schools. Includes info about research, programs, training courses, and parent education.

ConductDisorders.com

http://www.conductdisorders.com/

The creator of this Web site writes: "Many people ask how this Web site got started. I wish I had some wonderful story for you, but I was just like the hundreds of other parents out there, desperately searching for information to help my own son and his increasingly destructive behavior problems.

After many months of searching for information for his official diagnosis, Volitional Conduct Disorder, I began to realize how intertwined all these behavior disorders really are ... and how difficult finding good information was. But, the information began piling up and I thought I'd try to help other parents reduce the 'search time' by putting it all under one roof."

Coping with School Violence

http://www.familyeducation.com

A great selection of topics, polls, quizzes, downloads, discussions, printables, ask the experts, etc.

How to Find Help for Life's Problems

http://helping.apa.org/brochure/index.html

This online brochure comes from the American Psychological Association's consumer Help Center.

Just for Parents

http://www.schooltechnologies.com/parents/default.htm

A great selection of informative discussions about parenting decisions and advice for school, home, and the community. (School Technologies)

Middle School Malaise

http://helping.apa.org/family/malaise.htm

The transition from primary to middle school is stressful enough. Add the ingredients of adolescence and schools not designed to be stimulating and teen-friendly, and middle-school malaise can thrive. (APA)

NASS

http://www.safeschools.org/

National Alliance for Safe Schools. Nonprofit corporation that offers school safety and anti-violence workshops.

Networks: School Violence

http://www.ncvc.org/newsltr/schvio.htm

NCVC. .org. National Center for Victims of Crime. A great menu of safety strategies.

ParenthoodWeb—ASK THE PROS

http://www.parenthoodweb.com/parent_cfmfiles/articles.cfm/2

Search for articles on parenting, pregnancy, childcare, women's health, strollers, car seats, adoption, baby crying, infant sleep.

Parenting of Adolescents

http://about.com/parenting/parentingteens/mbody.htm

Here's an entire site devoted to the parents of teens, from early adolescence to college application and "Can I borrow the car?" time. (MiningCo)

Parent Resources

http://www.nncc.org/Parent/parent.page.htm

A collection of great articles on parent-child, family, and sibling relationships. Also *en español*. (National Network for Child Care)

Parents' Guide to the Internet

http://www.ed.gov/pubs/parents/internet/

Information on safely navigating the "information highway" at home and in school. Tips for getting started, a glossary of Internet terms, and a list of recommended sites. (U.S. Department of Education)

Parent Soup

http://www.parentsoup.com

This is one of the largest gathering places online for the parents of children and teens to learn and share information. Daily opinion polls, discussion.

ParentsPlace.com

http://www.parentsplace.com

Easy-to-access chat, bulletin boards, and special features, topics ranging from the terrible twos through teen years. A welcome focus on women's health and parental relationships.

PAVNET Online

http://www.pavnet.org/

A "virtual library" of information about violence and youth at risk, representing data from seven different federal agencies. It is a one-stop, searchable information resource to help reduce redundancy in information management and provide clear and comprehensive access to information for states and local communities.

Raising Children to Resist Violence: What You Can Do

http://helping.apa.org/family/raising.htm

From the American Psychological Association, basic strategies, suggestions, and information for parents.

Safe Schools

http://geocities.com/Heartland/Flats/3125/

Publishes a variety of school violence prevention and bus safety ideas and policy suggestions.

School Safety and Violence Prevention

http://eric.uoregon.edu/trends_issues/safety/index.htm

Research report discusses steps schools can take to prevent violence. Provided by the Clearinghouse on Educational Management.

School Violence

http://www.columbia.edu/~kmv4/page1.htm

Discusses the components of peace education which include: conflict resolution, multicultural education/curriculum, etc.

School Violence—Secondary School Educators Net Links

http://www.7-12educators.tqn.com/education/7-12educators/msub67schoolsafety.htm

Internet Resources on violence and drugs in schools.

Steps Parents Can Take to Stop School Violence

http://www.nwrel.org/comm/monthly/stepscanstop.htm

Discusses steps parents can take to stop school violence.

Stopping School Violence

http://www.ncpc.org/2schvio.htm

Discusses stopping school violence. A dozen things parents, students, teachers, law enforcement, principals, and the rest of us can do.

Student Violence in America's Schools

http://www.nytimes.com/learning/general/specials/schoolviolence/index.htm

A special presentation of the *New York Times,* featuring a database of information about incidents, articles on the social and legal issues, a discussion forum, and a guide to online resources about violence in schools.

The Teacher's Guide

http://www.theteachersguide.com/

Get lesson plans and thematic units, find tips on classroom management, visit educational organizations, and read articles on school violence.

Three Rivers Youth

http://trfn.clpgh.org/try/

Organization to help children damaged by severe poverty, neglect, violence, and abuse mend their lives by finishing school and attaining jobs.

Warning Signs

http://helping.apa.org/warningsigns/

The online companion guide to the acclaimed APA-MTV special aimed at teens.

Index

Acknowledgments

A very special thanks goes to my agent June Clark, who caught a glimpse of this book in my "Ask Dr. Erika" columns and encouraged me to write it. Her extraordinary vision and encouragement made me pour my empirical work spanning more than a third of a century into this book. Thank you, June.

Thanks also to Mary Jane Ryan, Editorial Director of Conari Press. She was able to boil the work down and focus it—on what all of us can and *must do to* prevent further outbreaks of youth violence. Thank you very much, Mary Jane.

And thanks also to Heather McArthur, Managing Editor of Conari Press, for all her support. And to Rebecca Carpenter for research.

Violence Proof Your Kids Now is a small but from-the-heart tribute to Sophie and Hans Scholl. Those two German college students made the extreme sacrifice in their fight against evil.

In 1942, in the midst of World War II, this sister and brother pair started a resistance movement against Adolf Hitler. When they were caught, tortured, condemned to death, and led off to be shot, Sophie said, "After all, somebody had to make a start. . . ."

Will *you* make a start in the war against youth violence?

To Our Readers

CONARI PRESS publishes books on topics ranging from spirituality, personal growth, and relationships to women's issues, parenting, and social issues. Our mission is to publish quality books that will make a difference in people's lives—how we feel about ourselves and how we relate to one another. We value integrity, compassion, and receptivity, both in the books we publish and in the way we do business.

As a member of the community, we sponsor the Random Acts of Kindness™ Foundation, the guiding force behind Random Acts of Kindness™ Week. We donate our damaged books to nonprofit organizations, dedicate a portion of our proceeds from certain books to charitable causes, and continually look for new ways to use natural resources as wisely as possible.

Our readers are our most important resource, and we value your input, suggestions, and ideas about what you would like to see published. Please feel free to contact us, to request our latest book catalog, or to be added to our mailing list.

2550 Ninth Street, Suite 101
Berkeley, California 94710-2551
800-685-9595   510-649-7175
fax: 510-649-7190   e-mail: conari@conari.com
www.conari.com